A FRIENDSHIP
LIKE NO OTHER

Other Books by William A. Barry, SJ

A FRIENDSHIP LIKE NO OTHER

Experiencing God's Amazing Embrace

WILLIAM A. BARRY, SJ

LOYOLAPRESS.
A JESUIT MINISTRY
CHICAGO

LOYOLA PRESS.
A JESUIT MINISTRY
3441 N. ASHLAND AVENUE
CHICAGO, ILLINOIS 60657
(800) 621-1008
www.loyolapress.com

Imprimi potest: Very Rev. Thomas J. Regan, SJ, provincial

Acknowledgments continue on page 203.

Jacket design by Beth Herman
Interior design by Maggie Hong

Library of Congress Cataloging-in-Publication Data
Barry, William A.
 A friendship like no other : experiencing God's amazing embrace / William A. Barry.
     p. cm.
 Includes bibliographical references.
 ISBN-13: 978-0-8294-2702-8
 ISBN-10: 0-8294-2702-3
 1. Spirituality. I. Title.
 BV4501.3.B374 2008
 248.4'82—dc22

                                                    2007041349

Printed in the United States of America
  09 10 11 12 13 14 15 Versa 10 9 8 7 6 5 4 3

To Marika Geoghegan,
who has taught me much about friendship

Contents

Acknowledgments

This is a book about friendship with God, and it could not have come to fruition without the encouragement of many good friends. I am grateful to the following people: Luiz H. Chang, SJ, Marek Janowski, SJ, Bienvenu Matanzonga, SJ, and Rui Nunes, SJ, who read and commented on the original manuscript as part of a reading course in spiritual direction at Weston Jesuit School of Theology; Marika Geoghegan, who read the first parts with care and gave me the impetus to make the book more user-friendly; Kathleen M. Foley, SND, who was so enthusiastic in her appraisal of the first draft; my provincial, Thomas Regan, SJ, who did me the honor of reading the whole manuscript one Sunday afternoon and writing an enthusiastic letter of support; my sister, Kathleen May, who read the final draft one chapter a day, responded with daily e-mails of praise, and caught some typos that spell-check missed; and parishioners, retreatants, and spiritual directors who listened to me over the past two years at Campion Renewal Center (Weston, Massachusetts), the Jesuit Spirituality Center at St. Charles College (Grand Coteau, Louisiana), the Dominican Center for Religious Development (Detroit, Michigan), St. Eulalia

Parish (Winchester, Massachusetts), the Ignatian Spirituality Centre of Montreal, and the Jesuit Center (Wernersville, Pennsylvania).

I want to thank the many men and women who do me the honor of seeking spiritual direction from me; I learn so much from them of God's ways. Over the years, readers have taken the time to write to me about the positive effect my writing has had on their relationship with God. Such letters have been music to my ears and given me great consolation.

I want to say a special thanks to three people who went far beyond the call of duty, and even friendship.

Bonnie Johnson read the first draft with great care and the skill of a seasoned editor and suggested the format for part 1—at a time when she was facing a second round of treatments for leukemia. Words cannot contain my gratitude for her enthusiasm for the project and her solicitude for what I wanted to do. Jim Martin, SJ, not only read the manuscript with care and attention to detail but also buoyed my spirits with his excitement over the book. Bob Doherty, SJ, and Bob Lindsay, SJ, my friends and companions at Campion Center, had the unenviable task of reading the manuscript twice, in its first draft and then in its penultimate form. Both made invaluable suggestions, gave me the kind of encouragement I needed, and were honest in their critiques. Jim Martin, Bob Doherty, and Bob Lindsay embody what all Jesuits are asked to be for one another: "friends in the Lord."

Finally, I express my gratitude to George Lane, SJ, president of Loyola Press, and Joe Durepos, acquisitions editor, who approached me on more than one occasion to publish this book with Loyola. It is nice to be asked. Heidi Hill made the book so much better with her suggestions and buoyed me with her enthusiasm for the material.

Introduction: What Does God Want?

In her evocative poem "Primary Wonder," Denise Levertov
writes:

> Days pass when I forget the mystery.
> Problems insoluble and problems offering
> their own ignored solutions
> jostle for my attention, they crowd its antechamber
> along with a host of diversions, my courtiers,
>   wearing
> their colored clothes; cap and bells.
>
>   And then
>   once more the quiet mystery
>   is present to me, the throng's clamor
>   recedes: the mystery
>   that there is anything, anything at all,
>   let alone cosmos, joy, memory, everything,
>   rather than void: and that, O Lord,
>   Creator, Hallowed One, You still,
>   hour by hour sustain it.

It is no wonder that we often prefer the "host of diversions" and "the throng's clamor," as the questions that arise when they recede are daunting indeed: How is there anything at all? Why does God sustain us? And how long will it last?

In this book, I will confront another daunting question: what does God want in creating us? My stand is that what God wants is friendship.

To forestall immediate objections, let me say that I do not mean that God is lonely and therefore needs our friendship. This is a romantic and quite unorthodox notion that makes God ultimately unbelievable. No, I maintain that God—out of the abundance of divine relational life, not any need for us—desires humans into existence for the sake of friendship.

This thesis may sound strange, because it runs counter to much teaching about God. To be honest, I questioned it myself when I first began to think it through. Mind you, I have been writing about prayer as a personal relationship for many years, maintaining that God wants such a relationship with us, and I have used the analogy of a personal relationship between two people to describe the developing relationship between God and us. But the notion that God wants our friendship did not easily follow. Whenever it reared its head, I shrugged it off as a fancy not to be taken seriously. After all, I had been raised with the standard catechism answer: "God made me to know him and love him and serve him in this world and to be happy with him forever in the next." As far as I can remember, no one ever interpreted this as implying that God wants my friendship.

But over the past few years, as my own relationship with God has deepened and I have listened to people talk about how God relates to them, I have become convinced that the best analogy for the relationship God wants with us is friendship. I began to use this kind of language in talks and articles and found that it resonated with others. I hope that you will find similar resonance and will trust your experience more fully. I can think of nothing that would please me more than to hear that you, and many others, have come to find God "better than he's made out to be," as my Irish mother once put it. I believe that God would also be pleased.

But in order for us to trust this experience of God as friend, we must move beyond our feelings of fear of God. The teaching that most older Christians received about God induced fear of God rather than the feelings invoked by the term *friend*. I still meet more people who fear God rather than feel warm and friendly toward God. Does the idea of friendship with God figure into your experience of religious teaching and worship? I suspect that it does not.

The idea, however, has an ancient heritage. It can be defended as orthodox, perhaps even as the best reading of the developing revelation of God contained in the Bible. I was encouraged to undertake this book, after a number of false starts, by reading Liz Carmichael's *Friendship: Interpreting Christian Love*, a scholarly book that shows that there is an enduring tradition of identifying *caritas* (love or charity) with friendship, and thus defining God as friendship.

Two examples of this tradition cited by Carmichael will suffice. Aelred, the twelfth-century English Cistercian abbot of Rievaulx, developed his own variant of John's "God is love" (1 John 4:16): "Shall I say . . . God is friendship?" A century later, Thomas Aquinas defined *caritas* as friendship with God. Both writers knew the text from the first letter of John in its Latin form: "Deus caritas est."

This notion of friendship with God seems to have waxed and waned throughout history. It is possible that preachers and teachers of religion fear that embracing the idea of friendship with God may lead to effacing the mystery and awesomeness of God, and so they hesitate to talk about it. But I am convinced, as is Carmichael, that this is an idea whose time has come, and none too soon for the future of our world—as I hope will become clear as we proceed. For one thing, fear of God has closed off a closer relationship with God in many people I have met, and they seem drawn by the notion of friendship. For another, friendship with God leads to a wider and wider circle of friends as we realize that God's desire for friendship includes all people.

As noted, much of our teaching about God has stressed fear of God. And why not? The psalmist writes: "The fear of the LORD is the beginning of wisdom" (Psalm 111:10). But the fear of the Lord extolled in the psalm is a far cry from the fear instilled by religious teaching, which leads people to keep their distance from God. The psalms surely were not written to keep people far from God, but just as bad news sells better than good in the media, so, too, hellfire and brimstone make for more compelling teaching and preaching. But God, I believe, is shortchanged by such teaching and preaching tactics, and so are we.

The emphasis on hellfire may have salutary effects on the spiritual life in the short haul, but it can be argued that the long-haul effects leave something to be desired, especially when the threats no longer seem to hold. Witness what happened to the practice, among Roman Catholics, of the sacrament of reconciliation (called confession prior to the Second Vatican Council): as soon as Catholics learned after Vatican II that they would not go to hell as easily as they had been taught and that confession was necessary only if they had committed serious sins, they drifted away from its use in huge numbers and have not returned, in spite of much hand-wringing on the part of bishops and priests and the real benefits that can come from a healthy use of this lovely rite. If fear is the principal factor used to enforce a religious practice, the practice will end when the fear is removed, and it will be difficult indeed to bring about its renewal.

Worse still, the emphasis on hellfire and brimstone gives God a bad name. One can read the Bible as a story of the progressive revelation of God—a God of compassion. Jesus' use of the tender word *Abba*—"dear Father"—for God is the culmination of this progressive revelation.

The "fear of the Lord" that is the beginning of wisdom is a healthy realization of God's awesomeness. God is fascinating and awe-inspiring, even terrifying, as the theologian Rudolf Otto put it. But suppose for a moment that God, who is Mystery itself—awesome, terrible, and unknowable—wants our friendship. Then the beginning of wisdom might be an acceptance of God's offer, even though accepting it proves to be daunting, challenging, and even a bit frightening.

What I hope you will find in this book is an invitation to engage in a relationship of friendship with God and in a dialogue with me. In the book, I do not provide answers so much as make suggestions and ask you to either try a suggested approach or reflect on your own experience in light of my suggestions. I hope that this will help you become a friend of God; the book will not attain my purpose if all you get out of it are ideas.

In part 1 of the book, I will first examine human friendship as the best analogy for what God wants with us, and then I will offer some exercises to help you determine if the notion of friendship fits your relationship with God or to motivate you to try such a way of relating to God. In part 2, I will provide meditations on questions and issues that I have had to confront as I have reflected on the conviction that God wants my friendship. I hope that they will be helpful to you as you confront your own questions. Finally, in part 3, I will take up the questions of where we find God and how we distinguish the influence of God's Spirit on our experience from other influences.

As we begin this spiritual journey together, let us pray this prayer of St. Anselm of Canterbury, which he made to God as he began one of his theological works, and which I used daily as I began writing this book:

> Teach me to seek you,
> and reveal yourself to me as I seek;
> for unless you instruct me
> I cannot seek you,
> and unless you reveal yourself
> I cannot find you.
> Let me seek you in desiring you;
> let me desire you in seeking you.
> Let me find you in loving you;
> let me love you in finding you.

PART I

Experiencing God's Desire for Friendship

» 1

The Meaning of Friendship

The dictionary defines a friend as "one attached to another by affection or esteem." Classically, according to Liz Carmichael, there are three grounds for friendship:

- A common mode of being—for example, because you are human, I want to be your friend
- Attraction to a good character—for example, I want to be your friend because you are a good person
- A desire to improve oneself—for example, I want to be your friend because I want to become good like you

Carmichael goes on to say that "'perfect friendship' is mutual relationship combining all three grounds" and notes that the Bible adds to this classical understanding the notion that

3

God creates human beings in God's own image "for friendship with himself and one another."

You may be helped in reflecting on the idea of friendship with God by thinking about your friendships with others. Who are your friends? What makes you say that they are your friends? You enjoy being with them, so you can say that one reason you call them friends is that they are likable. Another reason is that you trust them. You tell them things about yourself that you would not tell a stranger, or even an acquaintance. You know that they will not abuse what you tell them; they will not tell others the secrets you share with them or hold what you tell them against you or over your head as a threat. At the deepest level, you trust that they will remain your friends even when they know some of the less savory aspects of your past life and your character. You also trust that they will stick with you through thick and thin, through good and tough times.

I'm sure that you can spell out even more characteristics that mark your friendships. And at least some of these will also be true of the relationship God wants with you. Exploring the growth of friendship in more detail will help make this clear.

The Growth of Friendship

Let's reflect on how you came to be friends with the men and women you have just considered. First of all, something attracted you to these friends, and something in you attracted them. We do not make friends, ordinarily, with people whom we find unattractive. Now, attractiveness comes in a variety of packages. We can be attracted by looks, by charm, by warmth, by intelligence, by wit, by character, by public stance, by courage, and so on.

Sometimes people we initially find unattractive become attractive when we see them in a different light; for instance, when a friend speaks of the person's kindness or sterling character, or the person does something unexpected. When I entered the Jesuits, I found myself strangely at odds with one of my fellow novices. We were like oil and water. I did not like him; I was afraid of him, in fact. He did not seem any friendlier to me than I to him. Needless to say, we did not spend much time in each other's company, except when necessary. But years later, when we were thrown together in a large community, he did a kind thing for me that was totally unexpected. My attitude toward him changed dramatically. I took the time to get to know him, and I found that I liked him and liked to be with him. We became very good friends.

Given this initial, or eventual, attraction, what happens next? You spend time with the potential friend in order to get to know him or her. At first the conversation will be rather superficial as you feel each other out. You will speak of your job, your education, your neighborhood. But as the friendship develops, you will move to deeper and deeper levels of mutual self-revelation. You will speak not only about your job, but also about what you like about your job and what you dislike. You will talk about how you get along with different family members. You will, in other words, begin to speak of matters of the heart.

Eventually, each of you will want to know your effect on the other; whether you ask openly or more covertly, you want to know if the other person likes you, enjoys your company, and wants to know you even better. If both parties want to know each other better, then this initial period of exploration can be likened to a honeymoon. The newfound friendship is engrossing, with both parties wanting to spend a lot of time together to cement the friendship.

No friendship, however, remains in the honeymoon period forever. Friendship is always in danger, because we are all bedeviled by fears and self-doubt. Questions arise: "Will Joe still want to be my friend if he knows that I cheated to get into a better college?" "What will happen if I tell Ann about the way I failed a good friend three years ago?" "Mary seems to talk a lot about her friend Jim. Does she like him more than me? And what will she think of my feelings of jealousy?" "Can I tell John about my bouts of drinking and my need to go to AA meetings?" Moreover, as the honeymoon period winds down, you may begin to notice things about your new friend that you don't like. You get angry with her at times and notice that she seems to get upset with you. Can the friendship weather the storms of disappointment, of anger, of jealousy, of pettiness? Even more, can it weather the violent storms of real failure to understand and stand by each other? Any real friendship will have to confront these issues, as they come with the territory of being human and frail and fearful.

Friends who make it through the turbulence of the post-honeymoon period may now begin to think of making a life change or engaging in a project together. One obvious example is a couple who decides to marry and start a family. But others also come to mind. You and your friend may decide to work together on a political campaign, start a business together, plan a vacation for both of your families, or carpool to work or school. Your friendship has begun to become generative, to look beyond itself. You want to work together to make the world or some small part of it a better place.

Finally, friendship has to face the inevitability of sickness and death. One friend will go before the other into death. A friendship will deepen during times of illness, or it will regress, depending on whether the friends are willing to continue the process of self-revelation or not. It can be difficult to continue: the one who is suffering can hold back on revealing her pain and fear and anger because she does not want to burden her friend, and her friend can hold back for the same reason. When you are very sick, you can talk about little else than how you feel; it can become wearying after a while for both you and your friend. But there are rewards for continuing to share the burdens and joys of life even unto death with our friends. And, I suspect, the mourning after death is easier for those who have done so.

At least the survivor can rejoice that he was trusted to experience with the friend what she went through. And if the survivor is a Christian, he may experience the presence of the friend with the risen Jesus.

Personal Friendship as an Analogy for Friendship with God

We have just explored some of the stages in the growth of friendship between two people. I will maintain throughout this book that God wants a friendship that is at least analogous with this description of a developing friendship. Once we get over the kind of fear of God engendered by early training, we enter something like a honeymoon period with God. This is followed by a period of distance when we recognize how shamefully short we have fallen of God's hopes for us. The distance is closed when we realize that God loves us, warts and sins and all, and the friendship is solidified. We are able to be ourselves with God. Ultimately, we can become collaborators with God in God's family business. For Christians, this stage of collaboration in the family business is called discipleship, or friendship with Jesus of Nazareth. Finally, friendship with Jesus, as all Christians know, ultimately leads to facing with him his horrible death on the cross. In the next four chapters, I will offer exercises to give you a chance to see if the notion of friendship fits your relationship with God.

» 2

Friendship with God in the Bible

As we've discussed, the idea of friendship with God is not always easy to accept, whether because of past religious training or fear of God or distance from God. In order to better understand God's desire in creating the world, we can turn to the revelation of God in the Bible. I offer a few passages here that can be read as God's invitation to friendship; in reflecting on these stories from Scripture, you may find that you experience God asking you for your friendship, as the men and women in the stories did.

What Biblical Revelation Tells Us about God

The Jewish religion distinguished itself from other religions as the Israelites realized that the God they worshipped was not a tribal god—in other words, not just their god—but the creator of the universe, the only God there is and, therefore, the God of all people. We meet this God, the awesome One, Mystery itself, in the Hebrew Bible. It took some time for the implications of this revelation to sink in for the Israelites, but those implications were momentous.

Imagine yourself in the presence of this creator God, feeling that you have been wronged by a neighbor of a different religion and wanting revenge. As you pray for such revenge and imagine how you and God might obtain retribution for the wrong committed, it dawns on you that your neighbor is also a child of God. Such a realization must have been behind a story told by a rabbi in medieval times: There is a party in heaven after the Egyptian army has been destroyed and the Israelites saved at the Sea of Reeds (Exodus 14:15–31). The heavenly host notices that God is not joining the party but is weeping. They protest: "Why are you sad? Your people have been saved. The Egyptians have been destroyed." And God says, "The Egyptians are also my people."

One wonders how this story was received by the oppressed Jews of the rabbi's day. Did they react with anger? After all, in the Bible God threatens destruction on Israel's enemies. This rabbi's story seems to deny the truth of such threats and to crush hope that the people's persecutors would be destroyed. In addition, God is portrayed in the Bible as doing some disturbing and even horrible things. For example, God is pictured as carrying out the killing of the firstborn of Egypt (Exodus 12:29) and later ordering an ethnic cleansing when the Israelites come into the Promised Land

(Joshua 6:17, 21). This God seems to be a warrior who has friends and enemies. The people of the rabbi's time would have considered themselves friends of God, not enemies.

But there is something in the biblical revelation of God that could have led a medieval rabbi to tell the tender story of God's weeping over the destruction of the Egyptians. Perhaps the rabbi was moved in this direction by reflecting on the book of Jonah, in which God says to Jonah, "And should I not be concerned about Nineveh, that great city, in which there are more than a hundred and twenty thousand persons who do not know their right hand from their left?" (4:11). The Ninevites were pagans, not Jews, and Jonah expected their destruction, becoming petulant when God accepted the Ninevites' repentance and did not destroy them.

In the same way, I believe, there is something in the biblical revelation that can lead us to the conviction that God wants our friendship. I invite you to engage in a few prayerful exercises based on some of the biblical stories that might draw us to this conclusion.

St. Ignatius of Loyola, the sixteenth-century Spanish mystic and founder of the Society of Jesus (the Jesuits), invites those who use his *Spiritual Exercises* to pause before each prayer session and consider the following: "I will raise my mind and think how God our Lord is looking at me, and other such thoughts" (n. 75). Before each of the exercises here, imagine that God is looking at you, waiting for you to become aware of that look. During the course of these exercises, you may have some questions or objections. Keep them in mind. The meditations of part 2 address questions and objections. If yours are not considered there, you may find that you can discuss them with God and other believers.

The First Creation Story

In the first chapter of Genesis, creation is attributed to the one God. God speaks, and the world comes into being. Try to notice the exuberance in this story as you read: it reveals something about the creator God who calls us to friendship.

I was helped in my reading of the story by hearing Haydn's *Creation* sung in the original German. I was struck by the strength and joy of God's wish for living creatures: "Be fruitful and multiply." In the German, the bass telling the story sang, with gusto, "Mehret euch!" *Mehret* is a verb formed from the adverb *mehr*, which means "more"; *euch* is the reflexive pronoun *yourselves*. So God tells the living creatures, and later the first man and woman, "More yourselves." Now, this obviously is a call to propagate. But you can also hear more in the words: "Be more!" "Grow!" "Be all that you can be!" There is no hint of stinginess in this creation story, of God being careful or hedging bets. There is no sense, in other words, that God is afraid of having rivals in creativity.

As you ponder this scene, do you feel more attracted to God?

In the text, God then says: "Let us make humankind in our image, according to our likeness. . . . So God created humankind in his image, / in the image of God he created them; / male and female he created them" (Genesis 1:26–27). Let these words sink in. God wants us human beings to exist in this world. Moreover, we are made in God's image; we are made to be like God in this world. What does it mean to be like God? Perhaps we have a clue to the answer in what we have just noted about God's generous creativity.

In addition, one can understand God's command to "fill the earth and subdue it" (1:28) as a wish that human beings be God's stewards, God's aides, God's co-laborers in creation. This text has been used by generations of people to justify the rape of the earth, but a more generous reading of it seems more in keeping with the tenor of biblical revelation and the notion of friendship with God. By "generous reading," I mean recognizing that the biblical text is a human text trying to communicate something about the Mystery we call God. A generous reading realizes that the text is colored by the cultural biases and ignorance of the writer's time and yet has something true to say about God that has meaning for our time and for all time. An ungenerous reading sees only the inconsistencies and cruelties attributed to God or takes texts literally as revelations of God without considering the human recipients of the revelations.

A Christian might read this story as intimating that God is triune, because the text has God saying, "Let us make . . . " The Israelites, of course, did not think in terms of Trinitarian relations. But I want to note this Christian doctrine at this point, without inferring that the texts of Genesis themselves reveal God as triune, in order to indicate another way in which human beings are created in the image and likeness of God. We are relational creatures; we exist as persons only in relationship. And our first relationship, the one that constitutes us as persons, is with God. We will reflect more on the doctrine of the Trinity later in the book.

The Second Creation Story

Chapters 2 and 3 of Genesis contain a second creation tradition. It uses different imagery, but it, too, can be read as God's invitation to friendship. The story begins with the creation of one human being, "man" (*adam* in the Hebrew), who is placed in the garden "to till it and keep it." It is a garden of abundance where the man's every desire is fulfilled, with only one exception: he cannot eat of the tree of the knowledge of good and evil. In spite of the abundance, the man is lonely, and so God creates a soul mate for him, a "woman" (*issa* in the Hebrew). Haydn's *Creation* ends with a lovely duet in which the man and the woman celebrate their love for each other, followed by a recitative by the angel Uriel, who tells the couple that they will be happy forever, "unless unfaithful fancy tempt you to desire more than you have or know more than you should." The final chorus is a joyous song of praise to God.

Again, if we can read this story generously, without asking it to conform to our own sensibilities, we find a lovely image that may tell us something about why God creates human beings. Play with the garden image for a while. This universe is a garden of abundance where nothing is lacking. God is generous indeed. The only prohibition is against eating of the tree of the knowledge of good and evil, a small price to pay to live in such a wonderful place, and perhaps not a price at all, but just good sense. After all, why would anyone want to know the difference between good and evil if such knowledge could be avoided? Human beings are asked to live and toil in this garden, cooperating with God in the work of creation.

From what happens in chapter 3 after the man and woman have eaten of the forbidden tree, we can fill out the image. After a day of labor, God walks "in the garden at the time of the evening breeze" (Genesis 3:8). Imagine this scene as a regular occurrence. God and human beings, after a day of work, get together in the cool of the evening to shoot the breeze, as it were. This is an image of friendship and intimacy, of cooperation in creativity and in relaxation. Let yourself bask in this image—"inhabit it," as the British theologian James Alison would say. Notice how you react as you do.

If you experience some uplifting of the heart, some joy, some desire for "you know not what," as C. S. Lewis says, perhaps you are experiencing the deep desire of the human heart for friendship with God, which is the correlative of God's desire in creating us.

The story of the fall of the first human beings, in chapter 3 of Genesis, is written to explain what went wrong with the good world God created. Unlike the stories told by cultures surrounding Israel, which tended to blame a battle between gods and demigods for the evils and violence so evident to all, this story puts the blame squarely on human beings themselves, albeit abetted by the "serpent." It is interesting to note that the temptation that leads to the sin is the arousal of a desire for the forbidden fruit by the serpent, and that the desire is coupled with the wish to become like God. The first human beings let "unfaithful fancy tempt" them "to desire more than you have or know more than you should," the temptation Uriel warns them against in Haydn's *Creation*.

The only desire denied in the garden is the desire to know good and evil. In the Hebrew, "knowing good and evil" refers to coming to know or experience the difference between good and bad things. The only way one can do that is by tasting something bad and something good, by doing something bad and something good. This knowledge is not necessary for survival in the garden; one can get along quite well without it. But the serpent insinuates something that is foreign to God's creative enterprise—rivalry: "God doesn't want you to eat this fruit because God doesn't want you to be like God."

The lie at the heart of human sinfulness is that we can gain control of our existence by some action of our own and that God does not want us to have this power. The story of

God creating human beings in God's own likeness is contained in the first account of creation, but not in this one. However, the final editor of the book of Genesis knew the first account, because he included it in his book. Hence, he knew that human beings are already like God, because God wants this to be so; God has not set up a rivalry between God and any creature. Similarly, there is nothing human beings can do to ensure their continued existence; God is the only guarantor of that, just as God is the only creator. So instead of accepting the friendship with God that was offered, human beings chose to enter into rivalry with God. The consequences of that disastrous choice plague our world and us still.

It might be worthwhile to ponder another image prominent in this story. At the end of chapter 2 of Genesis, we read, "And the man and his wife were both naked, and were not ashamed" (2:25). However, when they had eaten of the fruit of the tree of the knowledge of good and evil, "the eyes of both were opened, and they knew that they were naked; and they sewed fig leaves together and made loincloths for themselves." In addition, when they heard God walking in the garden at the time of the evening breeze, they "hid themselves from the presence of the LORD God among the trees of the garden" (3:7–8).

Again I invite you to play with this image, to inhabit it. Before innocence is destroyed, the man and the woman are not ashamed of their nakedness before God or each other. One could take this nakedness for more than physical nakedness; it can stand for psychic and spiritual transparency before God and each other. But once their eyes are opened, they are ashamed and go into hiding. They are no longer transparent before God and each other.

God's call, "Where are you?" (3:9), can be read as an almost playful call of a father to a child, according to the Scripture scholar E. A. Speiser. God knows that they have been up to no good but still draws them into a personal relationship. Of course, they engage in the usual human folly of trying to put the blame on someone else. Their shame over their sin keeps them from resuming the friendship even when God wants to.

Abraham and Sarah

The next few chapters of Genesis can be read as the progressive effects of human foolishness. Cain kills Abel, humans live shorter and shorter lives, and incest and other abominations befoul the earth. Finally, in chapter 11, with the story of the tower of Babel, human beings reach the culmination of estrangement from God and one another: they can no longer communicate, because they do not speak the same language.

But God does not give up. God begins a new chapter in the long process of bringing us to an adult friendship by calling Abram and his wife, Sarai, to leave their ancestral home and found a nation whose ultimate purpose is to be a "light to the nations" (Isaiah 49:6) about who God is and what God wants.

We can read the story of the call of Abram and Sarai as one of growth in friendship. (It is interesting to note that Muslims refer to Abraham as "the friend of God.") The development of this friendship shows itself when God changes their names to Abraham and Sarah, a sign of their changed status in God's eyes, something like the giving of nicknames to our friends. But it shows itself even more in the way Abraham and Sarah grow in their ability to be more open and even humorous with God.

God promises that Abraham will have a son by Sarah. As time goes on, however, Sarah remains barren, so she gives Abraham her servant Hagar to bear his son, and Ishmael is born of Hagar. When God repeats the promise that Abraham will have a son by Sarah, "Abraham fell on his face and laughed, and said to himself, 'Can a child be born to a man who is a hundred years old? Can Sarah, who is ninety years old, bear a child?' And Abraham said to God, 'O that Ishmael might live in your sight!'" (Genesis 17:17–18). Abraham, in effect, is telling God to get serious—the only son Abraham will have is Ishmael. But God insists that Sarah will have a son, and as if in the spirit of Abraham's humor, God adds, "As for Ishmael, I have heard you; I will bless him and make him fruitful and exceedingly numerous" (17:20). In the next chapter, God repeats the promise that Sarah will bear a son, and Sarah, too, laughs. God asks Abraham, "Why did Sarah laugh?" to which Sarah replies, "I did not laugh." God replies, "Oh yes, you did laugh" (18:12–15).

Can you sense God smiling as he says this? There is a repartee in these lines that indicates an extraordinary level of intimacy.

The reciprocal nature of this intimacy shows itself in the next scene. On the way to see if things are as bad as reported in Sodom, God muses, "Shall I hide from Abraham what I am about to do . . . ? No, for I have chosen him, that he may charge his children and his household after him to keep the way of the LORD by doing righteousness and justice" (Genesis 18:17, 19). God then tells Abraham that if things are as bad as reported in Sodom, the city and all its inhabitants will be destroyed. Abraham remonstrates with God:

> Will you indeed sweep away the righteous with the wicked? Suppose there are fifty righteous within the city; will you then sweep away the place and not forgive it for the fifty righteous who are in it? Far be it from you to do such a thing, to slay the righteous with the wicked, so that the righteous fare as the wicked! Far be that from you! Shall not the Judge of all the earth do what is just? (18:23–25)

Abraham has come a long way indeed in his friendship with God: he can tell God how to be God! Moreover, God gets into the spirit of the exchange and engages in wonderfully amusing haggling with Abraham, which ends with God agreeing that the city will be spared if ten righteous people are found in it.

We can read these passages as an illustration of a developing friendship between God and human beings, a friendship that shows itself in humor and in a growing transparency on both sides. By establishing this relationship, the story tells us, God continues the quest to make human beings friends of God and, I might add, of one another. But we will have more to say on that point later.

How did you react to this story? Are you more drawn to engage in a relationship of friendship with God? Do you want to have the kind of friendship that Abraham and Sarah had with God?

The Descendants of Abraham and Sarah

The rest of the book of Genesis tells the story of the descendants of Abraham and Sarah. It is a story of a developing friendship with and alienation from God. The book ends with the long saga of Joseph and his brothers, in which Joseph is betrayed by his brothers and then, remarkably, forgives them, a story that tells us something of how this people grew in their understanding of who God is and who God wants them to be. By the end of the book, however, the chosen people are in Egypt, where, as we find out at the beginning of the next book, Exodus, they soon become enslaved and oppressed. What continues to be revealed through these stories is that God is on the side of the losers and victims of this world, choosing to befriend them and make them the light of the world.

In their better moments, the Israelites remember that they were chosen to be God's people not because they have redeeming qualities, but purely because God loves them:

> It was not because you were more numerous than any other people that the LORD set his heart on you and chose you—for you were the fewest of all peoples. It was because the LORD loved you and kept the oath that he swore to your ancestors, that the LORD has brought you out with a mighty hand, and redeemed you from the house of slavery, from the hand of Pharaoh king of Egypt. (Deuteronomy 7:7–8)

As you let these words touch you, you might find it helpful to change the word *loved* in this passage to *liked*. The theologian James Alison points out that the word *like* may better capture the kind of affection God has for us and the genuine pleasure God takes in our company.

Can you think of any other story of a people's founding that is so openly critical of the people, and even of their heroes? Virgil's great epic poem, the *Aeneid*, tells the story of the founding of the Roman people as a heroic saga of a fight against great odds. The people of the United States hear the story of the heroic revolution that established the "land of the free and home of the brave." But the story of the Israelites glorifies the wonders of God, who saved them in spite of themselves. They are depicted as ungrateful, cowardly, and fearful, wanting to go back to Egypt, where they were slaves, after God has miraculously rescued them and led them through the Red Sea.

> The rabble among them had a strong craving; and the Israelites also wept again, and said, "If only we had meat to eat! We remember the fish we used to eat in Egypt for nothing, the cucumbers, the melons, the leeks, the onions, and the garlic; but now our strength is dried up, and there is nothing at all but this manna to look at." (Numbers 11:4–6)

Later, on the edge of the Promised Land, they whine and whimper when scouts tell them that though the land is indeed flowing with milk and honey, it is defended by fierce people:

> Then all the congregation raised a loud cry, and the people wept that night. And all the Israelites complained against Moses and Aaron; the whole congregation said to them, "Would that we had died in the land of Egypt! Or would that we had died in this wilderness! Why is the Lord bringing us into this land to fall by the sword? Our wives and our little ones will become booty; would it not be better for us to go back

> to Egypt?" So they said to one another, "Let us choose
> a captain, and go back to Egypt." (Numbers 14:1–4)

As we read these stories sympathetically, we may recognize ourselves as brothers and sisters of these Israelites, for
we know that we are not heroes either, but often whiners
and losers, even after we have seen God's wonders in our
lives. Yet for some crazy reason, God chooses them and us to
be the bearers of the promise for the whole world.

Only a true friendship, a genuine liking, can explain
such crazy fidelity. How do you feel about God as you reflect
on these readings?

The continuing story of the Israelites in the
Promised Land is no better. Even their greatest king,
David, is revealed as an adulterer and a murderer. His son
Solomon begins wisely and develops a strong and pros-
perous nation but then dissipates everything in idolatry
and lust. Most of the other kings lead the people astray.
As a people, they are the prey of larger and mightier surrounding peoples and often enter into disastrous alliances
that lead to their impoverishment and destruction. The
final indignity comes when Jerusalem is captured by the
Babylonians, Solomon's great temple is razed, and many
of the people, especially the artisans and the upper class,
are led into exile in Babylon. It is the great disaster of
the Old Testament. The Israelites must have wondered if

God had given up on them. Perhaps we have experienced such a feeling.

But God did not give up on them. They were still the apple of God's eye, the people God chose to be the light of the world. The great prophecies of the second section of the book of Isaiah (chapters 40–55) were written while the people were in exile in Babylon. They show God as continuing to care for them, watch over them, and work in order to bring them back to the Promised Land.

The second section of Isaiah begins with the words "Comfort, O comfort my people." In chapter 43, Isaiah offers these bold statements, which must have been comfort to a people who were likely close to despair in exile:

> But now thus says the LORD,
>> he who created you, O Jacob,
>> he who formed you, O Israel:
> Do not fear, for I have redeemed you;
>> I have called you by name, you are mine.
> When you pass through the waters, I will be with
>>> you;
>> and through the rivers, they shall not overwhelm
>>> you;
> when you walk through fire you shall not be
>>> burned,
>> and the flame shall not consume you.

For I am the LORD your God,

the Holy One of Israel, your Savior.

I give Egypt as your ransom,

Ethiopia and Seba in exchange for you.

Because you are precious in my sight,

and honored, and I love you,

I give people in return for you,

nations in exchange for your life.

Do not fear, for I am with you;

I will bring your offspring from the east,

and from the west I will gather you;

I will say to the north, "Give them up,"

and to the south, "Do not withhold;

bring my sons from far away

and my daughters from the end of the earth—

everyone who is called by my name,

whom I created for my glory,

whom I formed and made."

(43:1–7)

God did not abandon them after all. God still wanted their friendship and remained true to the promises made to Abraham, Isaac, and Jacob. In these lines, God, out of faithful love, promises to bring the Israelites back home.

As you read these lines, do you hear them as directed to you? Can you imagine God saying to you, "You are precious in my eyes; I love you" even though you, too, have often failed to live up to your best hopes for yourself?

The Promised Messiah

The Israelites were released from their captivity and came back to the Promised Land. They rebuilt the temple and once again began living according to the covenant. But their fidelity to the covenant continued to fluctuate. Throughout their history of fidelity and infidelity, they reminded one another of God's promise of a Messiah (translated into Greek as "ho Christos," and thus into English as "the Christ"), the "anointed one" who would usher in the final age of God's triumph, and their own.

Christians believe that Jesus of Nazareth, a Jew of the first century of our era, is the fulfillment of that promise. Indeed, we have come to believe that Jesus of Nazareth is God made flesh, God incarnate. As the Gospel of John says, "For God so loved the world that he gave his only Son, so that everyone who believes in him may . . . have eternal life" (3:16). In the great prayer that John puts into Jesus' mouth the night before he dies, Jesus talks to his Father: "Father, the hour has come; glorify your Son so that the Son may glorify you, since you have given him authority over all people, to give eternal life to all whom you have given him. And this is eternal life, that they may know you, the only true God, and Jesus Christ whom you have sent" (17:1–3).

The knowledge meant is heart knowledge, the kind of knowing friends have of one another. This is the kind of knowledge God wants us to have. How do you react to such a statement? Does it attract you? Frighten you? Make you wonder if it could possibly be true?

To complete this short biblical tour, I would like to remind you of another saying of Jesus, from the Last Supper in John's Gospel. In chapter 15, Jesus uses the image of the vine and the branches to indicate how his disciples' lives are closely intertwined with his own. Then he says:

> This is my commandment, that you love one another as I have loved you. No one has greater love than this, to lay down one's life for one's friends. You are my friends if you do what I command you. I do not call you servants any longer, because the servant does not know what the master is doing; but I have called you friends, because I have made known to you everything that I have heard from my Father. You did not choose me but I chose you. And I appointed you to go and bear fruit, fruit that will last, so that the Father will give you whatever you ask him in my name. I am giving you these commands so that you may love one another. (John 15:12–17)

I believe that these words are meant not just for those disciples who ate with Jesus on the last evening before his death but also for all those who follow Jesus. And all human beings are included in the invitation to follow Jesus. We are all called to be "friends of God, and prophets" (Wisdom 7:27). Allow yourself to hear Jesus' words as addressed to you.

I hope that these reflective exercises have given you a sense of how intimate God wants the relationship to be. Moreover, I hope that it is clear that the term *God's people* refers to all human beings. There is only one God who creates the universe. God wants friendship with everyone.

How do you feel as you let these words wash over you? No matter what your reactions are, they can give you something to talk over with God, or with God's Son, Jesus. Engaging in such a conversation is how friendship with God develops, a topic to which we now turn.

» 3

The First Stages of Friendship with God: Attraction and Disturbances

Because I am a Jesuit, I have made the Spiritual Exercises of St. Ignatius of Loyola many times. I have also directed many people through the Exercises. By this I mean that I have followed Ignatius's guidelines for engaging in a relationship with God in an effort to better know God and follow the Spirit's leadings, and I have guided others through this process. *The Spiritual Exercises*, a classic of Christian spirituality, contains an ordered series of prayer exercises based on Ignatius's experience of being led by God into a deeper relationship with God. It is written as a manual for those who direct others through the Exercises. The progression through the full series of exercises entails, in its ideal form, a thirty-day retreat from ordinary activity, with four distinct stages of prayer and contemplation. Adaptations can easily be made, however, for individuals and groups who want to experience the Exercises in a shorter period of time.

After years of making and directing the Exercises and reflecting on the idea of friendship with God, I believe that I have discerned a developmental pattern that appears in both the Exercises and the experience of friendship as sketched in the first chapter of this book. In this chapter and the next, I want to develop this pattern with you and ask you to consider whether you have experienced anything like it in your own relationship with God. Through the exercises I offer here, I hope you will come to know God's desire for your friendship, if you haven't already, and enter into a deeper relationship with God. But first I want to address those of you who find it hard to believe in a caring and loving God.

Exercises for Those Who Are Fearful of God

Poor and abusive parenting leaves some people with an image of father or mother as someone to be feared; this image is easily transferred to God. Others have an image of a terrifying and threatening God because of teaching imbibed in childhood. For some such reason, Pierre Favre (Blessed Peter Faber), one of the first Jesuits, had a terrible image of God when, in 1529, he began rooming with Ignatius while both were studying theology at the University of Paris. For four years, Ignatius patiently worked with Pierre to get him ready to make the Spiritual Exercises. I presume that Ignatius was helping him trust in experiences of a caring and loving God whose plans are for our good, not a test that finds us wanting. Eventually, through what we might call pastoral counseling or spiritual direction, Pierre was ready to begin the Spiritual Exercises. He had the foundation of an experience-based trust in God's desire for his friendship that enabled him to fully engage with God.

If you fear God more than you are attracted to God, perhaps you can find a spiritual director who can give you the kind of help Ignatius gave Pierre. Trying one or more of the following exercises might also help you. Before beginning any of these exercises, spend a few moments telling God that you are afraid of him and wish you weren't. Just let God know of your fear in your own words, but also let him know that you want things to be different between the two of you.

Then, as one prayer exercise, do something you enjoy, such as walk in the woods, get out in the sunshine, or look at pictures of your children, grandchildren, or nieces and nephews. Whatever it is you like to do, do it with the hope that you will begin to associate the feelings connected with this activity with God, for these emotions and reactions are how God communicates with us.

A woman who was very fearful of God liked to look at children at play. After a time of doing this with the hope just mentioned, she felt that God delighted in the activity too; slowly she came to feel and believe that God enjoyed her delight in children and enjoyed sharing this activity with her.

Here is another exercise you can try: Think of someone you love and who loves you. As you do, remember that he or she was created by God, given life on this earth just as you were. Notice how you feel about God as you continue to reflect on God's generous creativity.

As a third exercise, try to imagine God saying to you the words of Isaiah quoted in the last chapter:

> Do not fear, for I have redeemed you;
>> I have called you by name, you are mine.
> When you pass through the waters, I will be with
>>> you;
>> and through the rivers, they shall not overwhelm
>>> you;
> when you walk through fire you shall not be
>>> burned,
>> and the flame shall not consume you.
> For I am the LORD your God,
>> the Holy One of Israel, your Savior.
> (43:1–3)

Later in the passage, God says, "You are precious . . . / and I love you." In your prayer, ask to hear God saying those words to you. Take some time to do this. If you begin to feel afraid of God, tell God you are afraid and ask to feel differently.

As a fourth exercise, ask to hear Jesus speak to you as he spoke to his disciples at the Last Supper:

> I do not call you servants any longer, because the servant does not know what the master is doing; but I have called you friends, because I have made known to you everything that I have heard from my Father. You did not choose me but I chose you. (John 15:15–16)

Can you hear Jesus calling you his friend? Just keep asking to believe that he is talking about you when he says those words.

Finally, I adapt a fifth exercise from *The Spiritual Exercises*. I mentioned earlier Ignatius's suggestion that you think of how God is looking at you, and other such thoughts, before beginning a prayer period. Ignatius presumes that God is always interested in us, always aware of us. Recently when I followed this long-forgotten advice, I found myself awed by the thought that God was waiting for me to be aware of the divine presence. Perhaps reflecting on this notion will help you believe in God's love for and interest in you.

The Attraction to God

Ignatius begins the process of his Exercises with a reflection on the "Principle and Foundation," a rather dry and catechism-like passage:

> Human beings are created to praise, reverence, and serve God our Lord, and by means of doing this to save their souls.

The other things on the face of the earth are created for the human beings, to help them in the pursuit of the end for which they are created.

From this it follows that we ought to use these things to the extent that they help us toward our end, and free ourselves from them to the extent that they hinder us from it.

To attain this it is necessary to make ourselves indifferent to all created things, in regard to everything which is left to our free will and is not forbidden. Consequently, on our own part we ought not to seek health rather than sickness, wealth rather than poverty, honor rather than dishonor, a long life rather than a short one, and so on in all other matters.

Rather, we ought to desire and choose only that which is more conducive to the end for which we are created. (*The Spiritual Exercises*, n. 23)

One can reflect on these words and come to the realization that they are true, but I do not think they have their desired effect without an experience of God, an experience that makes God supremely attractive. I believe that this abstract statement from *The Spiritual Exercises* is based on Ignatius's experience of God as the mysterious Other who creates us out of overwhelming and generous love and continues to sustain us at every moment of our lives.

Ignatius believed that all human beings have experiences of God's creative and sustaining love. If we pay attention to these experiences, we will find that during them we desire God with all our heart and, at the same time, feel an enormous sense of well-being. Caught up in this experience, we feel that everything and everyone pales in comparison. We want this Mystery more than we want anything or anyone else. We become—for the moment, at least—free of inordinate attachments to people and things, or "indifferent," as Ignatius says; we would not want to choose anything that would take us away from the object of this desire for "we know not what," the Mystery we call God. A long life, health, riches—these all pale in comparison to the Mystery we desire.

In chapter 2, we looked at some Scripture texts that might evoke an attraction to God. Recalling how you responded to those texts might give you a taste of this desire for "you know not what." For those of you who have been drawn to prayer or praise, try to remember one of those times. Can you recall where you were? What you were doing? Allow yourself to savor the moment in memory.

Was the experience something like this one, described in the novel *Innocent Blood*, by P. D. James?

> Philippa sat absolutely still in the silence, and there began to flow through her a sense of tingling delight, entrancing in its strangeness. Even the inanimate

objects in the room, the air itself, were suffused with this iridescent joy. She fixed her eyes on the geranium on the windowsill. Why had she never before realized how beautiful it was? She had seen geraniums as the gaudy expedient of municipal gardeners to be planted in park beds, massed on political platforms, a useful pot plant for the house, since it throve with so little attention. But this plant was a miracle of beauty. Each flowerlet was curled like a miniature rosebud on the end of its furred, tender stem. Imperceptibly but inevitably as her own breathing they were opening to the light. The petals were a clear, transparent pink, faintly striped with yellow, and the fanlike leaves, how intricately veined they were, how varied in their greenness, each with its darker penumbra. Some words of William Blake fell into her mind, familiar but new. "Everything that lives is holy. Life delights in life." Even her body's flux, which she could feel as a gentle, almost controlled, flow, wasn't the inconvenient and disagreeable monthly discharge of the body's waste. There was no waste. Everything living was part of one great wholeness. To breathe was to take in delight. She wished that she knew how to pray, that there was someone to whom she could say: "Thank you for this moment of happiness. Help me to make [my mother] happy." And then she thought of

other words, familiar but untraceable to their source:
"In whom we live and move and have our being."

Can you recall feeling anything like that at some time in your life? Perhaps you were looking at a child or a friend or a sunset. Such experiences, I believe, are instances of God's creative touch desiring us into existence for friendship; our hearts are moved, and we want what God wants—namely, friendship with the Mystery we call God.

This experience of God, who creates out of love and for love, underlies the abstract words of the Ignatian Principle and Foundation. If you pay attention to such experiences, you will recognize that you are being drawn into a closer relationship with God, into friendship. When you relish such experiences, you engage in something like a honeymoon period in your relationship with God—you want to be with God and to experience God's presence more and more. These experiences, reflected on and savored, provide the firm foundation upon which you and God can build a deepening friendship.

Disturbances in the Friendship

At some point in a friendship, one becomes aware that something is amiss, and the honeymoon period is over. In the case of friendship with God, I know at this point that God has created me for friendship and wants a world where human beings live harmoniously with God, with one another, and with the environment, but I realize that the world is not like this, and I have not lived up to God's dream, either—the world and I have fallen short of what God wants. A disturbance has been introduced into my friendship with God.

In chapter 2, we saw this in the second creation story, in which the first human beings eat the forbidden fruit in an effort to be like God. They become afraid, clothe themselves, and hide from God. They feel ashamed and unworthy of God's friendship and expect punishment. Have you ever felt this way as you became aware of God's presence?

In the Spiritual Exercises, the retreatant who begins to feel ashamed and unworthy of God's friendship is embarking on the stage Ignatius calls the First Week, a period of facing up to one's sins and failures and the sins and failures of our human world. The questions the retreatant faces are stark: "Does God still want my friendship after all my sins and offenses? Does God still love our human world, given the mess we humans have made of it?"

A word of caution is in order. The temptation could be to move immediately into a severe examination of our past life to see all our sins. We need to recognize, however, that we cannot see our own sinfulness. Sin creates a blind spot that keeps us from seeing the real nature of our sinfulness. For this reason, we need to ask God to reveal our sins to us, to reveal how God sees us and the world. To ask God, in trust, for such a revelation is almost impossible unless we have had an experience of God as caring and loving; hence, the need for the kind of "Principle and Foundation" experiences just mentioned.

But even with an experience-based trust in God, we find it difficult to ask for such a revelation. I can attest from experience that it is not as frightening as you might expect. Here are a few ways to go about it.

An exercise. Recall the last experience you had of God as friendly and close. Now tell God that you want to get back to that closeness. You can say something like this:

> I know that there is something wrong in our relationship. If there is anything I have done or said or left undone or unsaid, let me know. I feel that I have not lived up to the commitments of our friendship; if the residue of those misdeeds is getting in the way of our friendship now, please show me.

Then think of some period of time in your past, and let the memories flow, trusting that God will show you what you need to know. You can do this exercise a number of times, remembering various periods of your life. Don't be compulsive and try to cover everything. Just let the memories flow. God's Holy Spirit will do the work of reminding you of what you need to know and repent of.

As you become aware of where you have failed to live up to God's dream for you or where you have turned away from God's offer of friendship, speak to God. Notice how God reacts to your willingness to see yourself through God's eyes.

Isn't it a lot less threatening and belittling than when you examine your own past sins by yourself?

You may be wondering what I meant when I said that you should notice how God reacts to you. I am not talking about hearing the voice of God as though you were in the same room. You might hear a voice in your mind or heart saying something that sounds like God responding to you. Or you might recall some passage of Scripture or a few words from a homily or talk that seem to be an answer to your desire to hear from God. You may wonder whether such thoughts or words are just the product of your overactive imagination. But you need to remember that the only way God can communicate with you is through your imagination—and your memories, insights, and thoughts. The question of whether they are from God is one of discernment. In part 3, I devote a chapter to the process of discernment. If you feel the need, you can go to chapter 14 now and read about this process.

An exercise. As you become aware of your sins, you might want to hear God say to you these words of the prophet Isaiah:

Wash yourselves; make yourselves clean;
>   remove the evil of your doings
>   from before my eyes;
cease to do evil,
>   learn to do good;
seek justice,
>   rescue the oppressed,
defend the orphan,
>   plead for the widow.

Come now, let us argue it out,
>   says the LORD:
though your sins are like scarlet,
>   they shall be like snow;
though they are red like crimson,
>   they shall become like wool.
>   (1:16–18)

Your sins are washed clean, God is saying to you. Can you feel the healing and cooling water of God's forgiveness washing over you?

What happens when God washes us clean of our sins? God does not merely refrain from punishment but restores us to friendship. Let's look at two examples of how God forgives.

An exercise. In Luke's Gospel, Jesus responds to charges that he welcomed sinners and ate with them (15:1–2) with this story:

> There was a man who had two sons. The younger of them said to his father, "Father, give me the share of the property that will belong to me." So he divided his property between them. A few days later the younger son gathered all he had and traveled to a distant country, and there he squandered his property in dissolute living. When he had spent everything, a severe famine took place throughout that country, and he began to be in need. So he went and hired himself out to one of the citizens of that country, who sent him to his fields to feed the pigs. He would gladly have filled himself with the pods that the pigs were eating; and no one gave him anything. But when he came to himself he said, "How many of my father's hired hands have bread enough and to spare, but here I am dying of hunger! I will get up and go to my father, and I will say to him, 'Father, I have sinned against heaven and before you; I am no longer worthy to be called your son; treat me like one of your hired hands.'" So he set off and went to his father. But while he was still far off, his father saw him and was filled with compassion; he ran and put his arms around him and kissed him. Then the son said to him, "Father, I

have sinned against heaven and before you; I am no longer worthy to be called your son." But the father said to his slaves, "Quickly, bring out a robe—the best one—and put it on him; put a ring on his finger and sandals on his feet. And get the fatted calf and kill it, and let us eat and celebrate; for this son of mine was dead and is alive again; he was lost and is found!" And they began to celebrate.

Now his elder son was in the field; and when he came and approached the house, he heard music and dancing. He called one of the slaves and asked what was going on. He replied, "Your brother has come, and your father has killed the fatted calf, because he has got him back safe and sound." Then he became angry and refused to go in. His father came out and began to plead with him. But he answered his father, "Listen! For all these years I have been working like a slave for you, and I have never disobeyed your command; yet you have never given me even a young goat so that I might celebrate with my friends. But when this son of yours came back, who has devoured your property with prostitutes, you killed the fatted calf for him!" Then the father said to him, "Son, you are always with me, and all that is mine is yours. But we had to celebrate and rejoice, because this brother of yours was dead and has come to life; he was lost and has been found." (15:11–32)

This is the parable of the prodigal son. The son is prodigal in his folly, but the father is even more prodigal in his "folly," according to the wisdom of the time, and perhaps of all time.

In the peasant society of Jesus' day, the listeners would have been shocked at the younger son's request for his share of his father's wealth. In effect, he is telling his father, "I wish you were dead," because in that society he could receive his inheritance only after his father's death. The listeners would expect the father to react violently; he would, at least, slap his son's face, and possibly do worse. Jesus' audience would have reacted with dismay to hear the father agree to the request. They would then have listened in disgust as the father is further disgraced by his son's behavior, which would get back to the village rumor mill. As they heard of the son's decision to return to the father, they would have expected that the son would now get his just deserts. The father could legally kill him for what he had done; at the least, he would banish him from his sight, perhaps giving him a job as a servant, but never allowing him into the house. Instead, this father welcomes the son back into the family and throws a party for the whole village. The father makes it possible for the son to betray him again. Moreover, even the older son, who shows his true colors in his resentment, is shown the same prodigal love.

You might want to reflect on this parable as you become aware of your sins. Do you experience God as welcoming you in this prodigal fashion?

An exercise. Jesus himself provides another example of the way God forgives. In John's Gospel, we read that Peter three times denied being one of Jesus' friends during the Passion. After the Resurrection, Jesus appears to Peter at the shore of the lake. Three times Jesus asks Peter, "Do you love me?" Three times Peter responds, "You know that I love you." Each time, Jesus tells him to feed "my lambs," "my sheep" (21:15–17). In this tender way, Jesus does much more than tell Peter that he is forgiven and that Jesus will not hold his denial against him; Jesus invites Peter back into friendship and even gives him charge of his disciples. Jesus trusts Peter even though Peter has given no proof that he will not fail the friendship again. In other words, when Jesus forgives, there is no residue of mistrust. God risks being hurt again and again by forgiving us, because by that forgiveness we are restored to friendship and mutuality.

Many Christians, identifying with Peter, have been overwhelmed with wonder and happiness to realize that Jesus offers them intimate friendship and companionship even after they have offended him deeply. Do you feel the beginnings of such wonder and happiness?

These two Gospel stories underline what God's forgiveness really entails. God does not retaliate and even goes beyond not holding a grudge: God takes us back into intimate friendship, where we can offend again. Moreover, God entrusts us with responsibility for others' well-being in spite of our weak characters. This is the kind of forgiveness that leads us to want to be the person God believes we can be. It does not, however, make it impossible for us to fail again, and, indeed, we do fail again and again.

In *The Spiritual Exercises*, Ignatius advises those who have a deep sense of their own sinfulness to have a conversation with Jesus on the cross. That is, Ignatius invites us to imagine ourselves standing at the foot of the cross, knowing how often we have failed in friendship with God, and ask him how it is that he became like us in order to die for our sins. Ignatius adds: "A colloquy is made, properly speaking, in the way one friend speaks to another, or a servant to one in authority—now begging a favor, now accusing oneself of some misdeed, now telling one's concerns and asking counsel about them" (n. 54). Ignatius presumes, in this short note, that we can feel differently in our relationship with God—sometimes as an unworthy servant and other times as a friend, although unworthy.

Those who can, in imagination, look Jesus in the eye, knowing that he sees us just the way we are, and find love and forgiveness feel a great sense of relief. People who ask God to show them their sins discover, to their delight, that along with the shame and tears they experience for the way they have lived, they are freed of a tremendous burden. With a great sigh of relief they realize that God still loves them in their sinfulness and still wants their friendship. They have passed through the honeymoon period and the turmoil of realizing how far they have fallen short of what God wants, and they still feel loved and welcomed by God.

What about the World?

You and I are not the only ones who have fallen short of what God wants; the whole world seems to be on the road to hell, far from the bounteous garden God wants it to be. The history of the world, it seems, is a story of loss and decline, not one of progress. You may be wondering how God looks at this world now. The question sits close to our heart, even if not articulated: "Has God given up on our world?" I want to help you address this often unspoken fear lurking at the edges of our consciousness.

An exercise. Recall the last time you felt close to God. You want to feel God's closeness so that you can ask God to help you face your fears about the situation of the world and arrive at a deep belief that God still loves this world. Then you could read the newspaper and let the stories touch you. You may begin to feel sad or angry or deeply disturbed by what you read. Talk to God the Father or to Jesus about your feelings. Ask how God reacts to what you have been reading. Ask God to show you what you need to see and understand about the horrors that affect you as you read.

Once, in a class I was teaching, I began discussing the experience of being caught up in the feeling of great well-being and a strong desire for God. Members of the class recalled their own experiences of such a welling up of desire. A nun from Australia spoke up: "I work in the slum of a large city. Sometimes when I get home at night and start to pray, I am overcome with sobs of sorrow and heartbreak." The silence in the room was profound. I asked her if she would want such an experience again. She said that she would, but not as a steady diet. I said then, "I wonder if you are experiencing the sadness and heartbreak of God for what we have done to our world."

I have come to believe that the deepest movements of our hearts, when we are touched by the joys and sorrows of others, reflect the heart of God. Perhaps God's heart is broken at what we have done and are doing to one another. Perhaps some of your reactions to what you have been reading in the newspaper are a pale reflection of what God experiences.

Later in the book, we will take up the issue of what friendship with God means in the face of natural disasters that devastate the lives of so many people. I write this on the first anniversary of the tsunami that destroyed so many lives in East Asia, the beginning of a year of natural disasters that seem unparalleled, at least in my lifetime.

An exercise. Ask to be in the presence of God. Then, in your imagination, go with God to the scene at Calvary. Recall that the whole story of God's dream for our world now comes to a climax. God has chosen the Israelites to be the light of the world and the people from whom will come the Messiah, the anointed one of God, the Savior of the world.

Christians believe that Jesus of Nazareth is that Messiah. He has, in word and deed, shown what God expects in order for the dream of God to come to fulfillment. Now God's own people have turned Jesus over to the pagan Romans to be crucified. In other words, both Jews and Gentiles conspire to destroy God's hope, Jesus of Nazareth.

Crucifixion is a horrible way to die. God sustains this world as the horror unfolds. Ask for God's reactions. Listen to the words of Jesus as he dies this horrible death: "Father, forgive them; for they do not know what they are doing" (Luke 23:34). Perhaps these words give us some indication of God's attitude to this broken and fallen world. If God did not give up on the world after this horror, then perhaps it is true that God will never give up on the world.

I hope that you have entered deeply into intimate friendship with God through these exercises and have come to know God's desire for your friendship, a desire that has not been deflected by your sins and failures or by the sins and failures of humanity in general. In the next chapter, I want to carry this notion of friendship with God forward through some reflections and exercises on the relationship with Jesus of Nazareth.

» 4

Going Deeper in Friendship with God:
Coming to Know Jesus as a Friend

If you have entered into a relationship of intimacy with God, you may now notice a change in your desire. You may begin to want to engage more cooperatively in the divine purpose of creation. If you are a Christian, perhaps you want to know Jesus—in whose eyes you saw forgiveness and love—more intimately in order to love him more ardently and follow him more closely, which Ignatius posits as the desire of the Second Week of the Spiritual Exercises. If this is your desire, you want Jesus to reveal himself, to let you know what makes him tick, what he loves and hates, what he dreams. Such revelation is the necessary condition for falling in love with him and wanting to follow him. In terms of the developmental scheme of friendship outlined in the first chapter, those who have come this far in their relationship with the Lord enter a stage of generativity.

This stage has its ups and downs, as it becomes clearer what being a companion of Jesus entails. After all, if we become his companions, we are liable to meet the same obstacles and enmity he met and suffer the same fate. So at this stage, we experience both an attraction to Jesus and his way of being human and a resistance. Those who persevere in the growing friendship with Jesus find themselves becoming freer of the attachments that prevent them from following the way of Jesus, from joining him in pursuing God's project in this world.

Coming to Know Jesus through Contemplation of the Gospels

If you are experiencing the desire to know Jesus more intimately now that you have experienced healing and forgiveness, you can begin with some contemplation of the Gospels. Contemplation, as Ignatius means it, is a rather simple way of using the Gospels for prayer. You begin each period of prayer by expressing your desire to know Jesus more intimately in order to love him more deeply and follow him more closely. Then you read a passage of the Gospels and let it stimulate your imagination in the way a good novel can.

People have different kinds of imaginations. Some are able to make something like a movie of each scene. They watch and listen as the scene unfolds in their imagination. I do not have that kind of imagination. I don't see anything, for the most part. My imagination is not pictorial; I seem to intuit the story or feel it. I was helped in understanding and trusting my imagination by realizing that I have visceral reactions to stories—I wince when I hear of someone hitting his finger with a hammer, and I weep when I hear people's stories of pain and loss. Each of us needs to be content with and trust the imagination we have. In contemplating the Gospel stories, don't be afraid to let your imagination go.

The Gospels are stories written to engage our imaginations, hearts, and minds so that we will come to know, love, and follow Jesus. They are meant to elicit reactions and, ultimately, a faith that shows itself in action. They are not biographies or historical documents or theological discourses.

As you begin to contemplate the Gospels with the hope of getting to know and love Jesus more, it is important to remember that Jesus of Nazareth was a historical human being who was born in a small territory in Palestine controlled by the Roman Empire. It is difficult for many Christians to take seriously that Jesus was a real human being because of the training and teaching they have had. They can say that Jesus was fully human, but the emphasis of most catechetical training and preaching has been on his divinity. And, to be truthful, many Christians think that calling Jesus divine means that he knew everything, including the future; that he always knew what others were thinking, because he could read minds; and that he could do anything he wanted

When we use our imagination in the contemplative way Ignatius suggests, we trust that God's Spirit will use it to reveal something important for us about Jesus so that we will love him and want to follow him. The only way that we can get to know another person is through revelation; the other must reveal him- or herself to us. In contemplating the Gospels, we are asking Jesus to reveal himself to us.

Examples of Contemplation of the Gospels

In the Second Week of *The Spiritual Exercises*, Ignatius gives two models of what he means by contemplation. A few points drawn from these exercises may help you understand what he recommends.

The first story from the Gospels presented for contemplation is that of the Incarnation. The text in Luke's Gospel says, "In the sixth month the angel Gabriel was sent by God to a town in Galilee called Nazareth" (1:26). Ignatius shows how his own imagination was moved by the words of Scripture: he imagined a conversation in heaven in which the Trinity looks down on the whole world and, seeing it in such sad shape, decides to send the Son. Scripture says nothing about such a heavenly conversation, but the words *was sent by God* impelled Ignatius's imagination in that direction. You, too, can let the words touch your imagination, hoping that in this way you will learn something about the ways of God.

Here is Ignatius's first suggestion for contemplating the Incarnation:

I will see the various persons, some here, some there.

First, those on the face of the earth, so diverse in dress and behavior: some white and others black, some in peace and others at war, some weeping and others laughing, some healthy and others sick, some being born and others dying, and so forth.

Second, I will see and consider the three Divine Persons, seated, so to speak, on the royal canopied throne of Their Divine Majesty. They are gazing on the whole face and circuit of the earth; and they see all the peoples in such great blindness, and how they are dying and going down to hell.

Third, I will see Our Lady and the angel greeting her. Then I will reflect on this to draw some profit from what I see. (*The Spiritual Exercises*, n. 106)

In his second and third suggestions, Ignatius invites the retreatant to listen to what the people are saying and consider what they are doing. Ignatius is giving your imagination carte blanche to engage with the text. Try it and see what happens. If you feel the urge, talk to Mary or Joseph and ask them to help you grasp what is happening. Talk with Jesus or with God the Father. At the end of each period of prayer, take a few minutes to reflect on what has happened and perhaps jot down some notes. You can go back to the same contemplation on another occasion to determine if there is more to see and hear and learn.

In the second contemplation, on the Nativity, Ignatius tells the retreatant to imagine where it took place: "Here it will be to see in imagination the road from Nazareth to Bethlehem. Consider its length and breadth, whether it is level or winds through valleys and hills" (*The Spiritual Exercises*, n. 112). He does not give a description of the terrain, although he had been to the Holy Land; instead, Ignatius leaves it up to the imagination of the person. Artists throughout history have used their imaginations to paint scenes of the Gospels, most of the time using the scenery and people they were familiar with as models. And many, like Rembrandt and Caravaggio, painted themselves into the scenes depicted. This is the kind of imagination Ignatius encourages.

We can also glean an understanding of the way contemplation works from Ignatius's own experience of contemplating the Nativity. He extols the poverty of the holy family, yet because of his own social background (he was born into a noble Basque family), he cannot conceive that Mary would not have a maidservant along to help her, although that would be highly unlikely in the historical circumstances. Thus, in the first point of the contemplation on the Nativity, he writes:

> This is to see the persons; that is, to see Our Lady, Joseph, the maidservant, and the infant Jesus after his birth. I will make myself a poor, little, and unworthy slave, gazing at them, contemplating them, and

> serving them in their needs, just as if I were there,
> with all possible respect and reverence. (*The Spiritual
> Exercises*, n. 114)

This kind of contemplation encourages each of us to let our imagination go. A pediatrician I know helped Mary deliver Jesus; a young Jesuit played a drum for the infant Jesus; an expectant mother received the infant Jesus from the hands of Mary.

After these two contemplations, Ignatius is quite sparing in his suggestions, because he does not want to get in the way of the person making the Exercises, nor does he want the one giving the Exercises to interfere. The one giving the Exercises should, writes Ignatius, "allow the Creator to deal immediately with the creature and the creature with its Creator and Lord" (*The Spiritual Exercises*, n. 15). I encourage you to use the Gospel stories as a vehicle for Jesus to reveal himself to you. And remember to beware of jumping too quickly to thoughts of Jesus' divinity. Let his humanity reveal to you who God is and how God wants you to live your human life as an image of God.

Jesus as a Difficult Friend

As you get to know and love Jesus, you will notice that he meets you in unexpected ways. Jesus can be a difficult friend, one who challenges and makes demands as well as supports and comforts. At times, you may want to tell him things like "I can understand why so many of your disciples left you. You're too much. It would be absurd for me to try to live the way you lived." You may well understand his family's concern that he was crazy (see Mark 3:21) and the religious leaders' belief that he was possessed by a demon (see Mark 3:22).

The only way forward in this friendship is to tell Jesus what you really feel and think and then wait for his response. Jesus responds in different ways to different people. Some have vivid imaginary conversations in which Jesus says surprising things. For example, one man who was struggling with an addiction asked Jesus to remove it. He heard Jesus say, "I can't. But we can overcome it together." For others, a phrase from Scripture that comes to mind may feel like an answer to prayer. Sometimes the response comes later in the day or week as an "aha" experience that brings closure to a situation or shows a way to move forward.

Most people who walk with Jesus in this contemplative way come to realize that following him is demanding and challenging. He promises nothing but his friendship and a share in his project. We see this in Mark's Gospel: at one point, Peter responds to Jesus' question "Who do you say that I am?" with "You are the Messiah" (8:29). Jesus responds with a hard teaching:

> Then he began to teach them that the Son of Man must undergo great suffering, and be rejected by the elders, the chief priests, and the scribes, and be killed, and after three days rise again. He said all this quite openly. And Peter took him aside and began to rebuke him. But turning and looking at his disciples, he rebuked Peter and said, "Get behind me, Satan! For you are setting your mind not on divine things but on human things."
>
> He called the crowd with his disciples, and said to them, "If any want to become my followers, let them deny themselves and take up their cross and follow me. For those who want to save their life will lose it, and those who lose their life for my sake, and for the sake of the gospel, will save it. For what will it profit them to gain the whole world and forfeit their life? Indeed, what can they give in return for their life? Those who are ashamed of me and of my words in this adulterous and sinful generation, of them the Son of Man will also be ashamed when he comes in the glory of his Father with the holy angels." (Mark 8:31–38)

A difficult friend indeed. As you contemplate texts such as this one, you will have various reactions, some of which you may not like. Don't be afraid of any of your reactions. Just talk with Jesus about them. You may also want to talk with other characters in the scene to get their take on Jesus. For example, you could ask Peter why he responded as he did to Jesus' prediction of his passion and how he felt after the tongue-lashing he got from Jesus.

Getting to know Jesus can be discomfiting, to say the least. Mark's Gospel gives us an example of how disconcerted a person can become. Shortly after the previous scene, a young man runs up to Jesus and asks, "Good Teacher, what must I do to inherit eternal life?"

> Jesus said to him, "Why do you call me good? No one is good but God alone. You know the commandments: 'You shall not murder; You shall not commit adultery; You shall not steal; You shall not bear false witness; You shall not defraud; Honor your father and mother.'" He said to him, "Teacher, I have kept all these since my youth." Jesus, looking at him, loved him and said, "You lack one thing; go, sell what you own, and give the money to the poor, and you will have treasure in heaven; then come, follow me." When he heard this, he was shocked and went away grieving, for he had many possessions. (10:17–22)

Because of this man's addiction to his possessions, he could not follow through on his desire to do more. Notice that he goes away grieving: he knows that he is losing something precious. How do you feel as you contemplate this scene?

You may occasionally find yourself feeling something like what this rich man felt. You, too, may want to follow Jesus completely but feel that something is standing in the way. You know that a total commitment to Jesus means sacrificing something in your life that you believe you cannot do without. What are you to do? After I gave a talk on prayer, a professor engaged me in this dialogue:

"I want a closer relationship with God, but I know that if I do get close to God, I will have to do something I do not want to do."

"Why don't you tell God that you don't want to do it?"

"Can I do that?"

"We are talking about a friendship here. You can tell God anything in your heart and then see how God responds."

That's the advice I would give you, too. Anything that comes up in these contemplations is grist for the mill of your relationship with Jesus. Remember that friendship develops through mutual transparency.

Does Jesus love the rich man any less when he goes away? Does he love the professor any less because he's stuck? If you have gotten to know Jesus, you will have an answer, I'm sure. For my part, I do not believe that Jesus loved the rich man any less, but I do believe that Jesus was disappointed.

I suspect, however, that his disappointment stemmed from the fact that the man would not continue the dialogue but walked away. If he had stayed with Jesus, he might have been able to say, "I cannot give up my wealth, but I wish that I could. Help me." That would have continued the conversation, and the friendship would have grown. You might want to extend your contemplation of the Gospel by going on to the following verses, where Jesus expresses his astonishment at how hard it is for those with riches to enter the kingdom of God.

Contemplating Jesus' Passion and Death

Contemplation of the Gospels with the desire to know Jesus better, love him more ardently, and follow him more closely leads inevitably to the Crucifixion. When we walk with Jesus to Jerusalem, we find ourselves wanting to share in his passion and death, and perhaps dreading it. We are ready to enter what Ignatius calls the Third Week of the Spiritual Exercises. Again we are asking Jesus to reveal himself, but this time we are seeking the hard revelation of what it was like for him to go through this terrible week trusting in his Father when he had no one else in whom to trust. This revelation is difficult because it is painful to see Jesus, who has by now become a close friend, go through this agony, abandoned by his friends, betrayed by one of them, accused by the leaders of his own religion of leading the people astray, and flogged, mocked, and hung naked on a Roman cross to die a horrible death.

Those who contemplate these scenes often find themselves resisting the revelation they desire. They may focus on all the other characters in the scenes rather than on Jesus. They may find themselves angry with God for allowing this horror. But if they continue to ask Jesus to reveal himself, they will find themselves drawn into a deeper love for him and a deeper sympathy. One woman I directed wept with relief when Jesus finally died. Contemplation of Jesus on the cross brings a heavy load. But just as it is consoling to share the pain of a friend's illness and death, it is consoling to share Jesus' pain and suffering and loneliness.

It can also be harrowing, as we see all our illusions about God being destroyed. Jesus experiences God's powerlessness to preserve him from this horror. Our own often unconscious image of God as one who saves the good from such a fate, who intervenes to strike down our enemies, is dashed. This experience, too, however, can be an opportunity for a deepening of our friendship with God. If we continue on the path of mutual transparency, we may see the truth of this observation made by Rowan Williams, the archbishop of Canterbury:

> We need . . . to see the Father's weakness and powerlessness as the inevitable and necessary corollary of the Son's powerlessness in a world of corrupt and enslaving power. . . . "God" vanishes on the cross:

Father and Son remain, in the shared, consubstantial
weakness of their compassion.

In the last sentence, Williams puts the word *God* in quotation marks because the "God" who vanishes is the illusory
"God" of those like Caiaphas (and us, if we are honest) who
believe in a God whose power is coercive and vengeful to
opponents or sinners.

Contemplating the Resurrected Jesus

Facing the full impact of Jesus' humiliating and painful
death on the cross is the only way to experience the real
joy of the Resurrection. In the final stage of the Spiritual
Exercises, the Fourth Week, one asks to share the joy of
Jesus resurrected from the dead, but the depth of that shared
joy comes only after sharing with Jesus something of what
he experienced in his crucifixion.

The risen Jesus tells the two disciples on the road to
Emmaus, "Was it not necessary that the Messiah should suffer these things and then enter into his glory?" (Luke 24:26).
I take this not as an eternal decree of God, but as a statement
that to be the Messiah he now is, he had to go through this
suffering. He still has the wounds, even in glory; the horror is not undone by the Resurrection. Rather, with the
Resurrection we find that his crucifixion and death are not
the last word. Here is a magnificent sign of God's forgiving

love: God, in Jesus, received the worst we humans could devise and did not retaliate by annihilating us. Even the worst we can do will not deter God from the desire to embrace us in friendship.

The joy of the Resurrection is that Jesus is alive and well, that God has raised him bodily from the dead, and that his resurrection will be ours. When you are given the grace to share in Jesus' joy through contemplation of the scenes of his resurrection, you can never despair, no matter what happens in your life, because you know in your bones that Jesus is risen and that you are one with him and will share in his resurrection.

If you have come this far in your friendship with Jesus, you now want to experience his joy, the joy he wants all his friends to share. Just as in the other stages of growth in friendship with Jesus, tell him of your desire to share his joy, to know him now in glory in order to love him more and be like him. Then contemplate some or all of the Gospel scenes of the Resurrection and let them touch your imagination. See what happens to you as you enter imaginatively into these stories of great joy after the harrowing loss of "God" experienced at the cross.

In the third book of J. R. R. Tolkien's *Lord of the Rings* trilogy is a scene that conveys something of the joy experienced by Jesus' disciples when the resurrected Jesus appeared to them. The realm of the Dark Lord Sauron has been destroyed, and against all hope the world has been saved, at least for the time being. Frodo, the hobbit, or half-ling, and his faithful servant and friend, Sam, have also been saved. Sam wakes up, smells wonderful perfumes, and sees Gandalf, the wizard he thought was dead. Sam says:

"Gandalf! I thought you were dead! But then I thought I was dead myself. Is everything sad going to come untrue? What's happened to the world?"

"A great Shadow has departed," said Gandalf, and then he laughed, and the sound was like music, or like water in a parched land; and as he listened the thought came to Sam that he had not heard laughter, the pure sound of merriment, for days upon days without count. It fell upon his ears like the echo of all the joys he had ever known. But he himself burst into tears. Then, as a sweet rain will pass down a wind of spring and the sun will shine out the clearer, his tears ceased, and his laughter welled up, and laughing he sprang from his bed.

"How do I feel?" he cried. "Well, I don't know how to say it. I feel, I feel"—he waved his arms in the air—"I feel like spring after winter, and sun on the leaves; and like trumpets and harps and all the songs I have ever heard!"

As you contemplate the scenes of Jesus' appearance to his disciples, perhaps you will feel something akin to what Sam feels after his and Frodo's desperate and seemingly fruitless journey to Mount Doom.

How are you feeling about your relationship with Jesus? Do you know him better and like him more? Does he know you better and like to be with you? I was deeply moved during a province retreat when Kenneth Hughes, SJ, one of the retreat leaders, had us imagine someone meeting Jesus after death. The person says to Jesus, "I wish I had known you better in life." Jesus replies, "I wish I had known you better." Imagining that scene was life-changing for me.

I hope that through these contemplations on the life, death, and resurrection of Jesus you have come to know him as a friend and have committed yourself to live according to his way of being human.

» 5

The Spirit and the Community of God's Friends

Conditioned as I am by *The Spiritual Exercises*, which says little explicitly about the Spirit, I initially included nothing in the book about friendship with God the Spirit. In this, of course, I am no different than most Christians, for whom the Spirit is the forgotten or least adverted-to Person in the one God. It was when I was nearing the end of writing this book that I became aware in prayer of something missing and realized that I had not included exercises related to experiencing the activity of the Spirit, the ongoing activity that draws all human beings into friendship with God, with one another, and with the whole created universe.

In the Gospels, we read of the Spirit a number of times. The angel Gabriel assures a perplexed Mary, "The Holy Spirit will come upon you, and the power of the Most High will overshadow you: therefore the child to be born will be holy; he will be called Son of God" (Luke 1:35). Matthew also attests to the same tradition: "Mary . . . was found to be with child from the Holy Spirit" (1:18); in a dream, an angel assures Joseph that "the child conceived in her is from the Holy Spirit" (1:20). Matthew, Mark, and Luke all say that the Spirit led or drove Jesus into the desert after his baptism in the Jordan. Luke writes, "Jesus, full of the Holy Spirit, returned from the Jordan and was led by the Spirit in the wilderness" (4:1), where he was tempted by the devil. After describing the temptations and Jesus' responses, Luke says, "Then Jesus, filled with the power of the Spirit, returned to Galilee" and began his public ministry (4:14–15).

Clearly the Gospel writers believed that Jesus was empowered by God's Spirit in his life and ministry. John's Gospel tells us that Jesus promised that the same Spirit would come upon his disciples after his death (14:15–17, 25–27; 16:12–15). In Luke's Gospel, the risen Jesus, just before his ascension, says to his disciples, "And see, I am sending upon you what my Father promised; so stay here in the city until you have been clothed with power from on high" (24:49). Luke's companion volume, the Acts of the Apostles, makes clear that this "power from on high" is the Holy Spirit. In John's Gospel, the handing on of the Spirit occurs on Easter night when Jesus breathes on this lost and hopeless group.

I propose that you take time to contemplate some scenes of this outpouring of the Spirit with the desire to become aware of the same outpouring on you, and on all of us. As noted earlier, God's desire for your friendship includes a desire for the friendship of every person created and a desire that they become a community of friends. If we want to grow in friendship with God, we need also to grow in our ability to embrace more and more of God's other friends—in other words, to become the church.

The Upper Room

We can begin our contemplation of the Spirit with the scene in the upper room in John's Gospel (20:19–23). Allow yourself to sense what it was like for those disciples as they cowered in the room in fear, and perhaps in hopelessness. How do they interact with one another? Imagine yourself with them before and after Jesus enters the room.

It may help you to know that in telling this story, John makes an allusion to the first creation story in Genesis. There we read that "the earth was a formless void and darkness covered the face of the deep, while a wind from God swept over the face of the waters" (1:2). The Hebrew word translated as "wind" can also be translated as "breath" or "spirit."

In the upper room at this moment of the disciples' darkness and hopelessness, Jesus "breathed" on them. John suggests that a new creation is beginning: "Jesus said to them again, 'Peace be with you. As the Father has sent me, so I send you.' When he had said this, he breathed on them and said to them, 'Receive the Holy Spirit'" (20:21–22). What happens to the disciples and to you as you imagine this scene?

Once, a colleague and I were asked to facilitate a meeting of a community of male religious who needed to make some decisions about their future living arrangements. They wanted to make these decisions with the help of the Holy Spirit. At the opening session, we proposed that they take some time for prayer about their hopes and dreams for the community and afterward come together in small groups to talk about what had happened when they prayed. It was clear as we listened to the different groups that these men were angry and suspicious of one another; hence, they did not trust this process of decision making. My colleague and I were stunned at the amount of anger and mistrust in the group. We did not have time to discuss with each other how to proceed. From nowhere, it seemed, I thought of the scene in the upper room before Jesus entered. I took it as an inspiration of the Spirit and said something like this:

> I have just been thinking of the scene in the upper room in John's Gospel. I can imagine how those men and women felt, especially the men who had denied and abandoned Jesus. All of them must have felt some sense of hopelessness. The one whom they had believed to be the Messiah had died a cruel death. What a disappointment! No doubt anger was present, and they did not

know what to do with it. Perhaps they began to point fingers: "At least I didn't deny I knew him." "I went with the women to the cross; where were the others?" At any rate, you can see that they might have had some of the emotions that you have experienced and expressed this evening. If you have some time before tomorrow morning's meeting, contemplate this scene with your own experience of this evening in mind. Ask Jesus to come into your midst as he came into the midst of the first disciples. Tomorrow morning we can tell one another what happened.

The next day, most of the community returned, but the atmosphere had changed.

As they spoke, they no longer tried to blame others for the state of things in the community. Each one took personal responsibility for some of the difficulties, and each one expressed hope that with the presence of the Spirit they could work together to resolve their problems and make some needed community decisions. Their contemplation of Jesus breathing the Spirit on them had effected some kind of transformation in the group. They moved toward becoming a community of brothers in the Lord. Perhaps this story will remind you of a similar situation in your life that makes this contemplation personal. In your church or your community, have you experienced Jesus breathing the Spirit on you?

Pentecost

You may next want to contemplate the scene of Pentecost, as described in chapter 2 of Acts. Notice what the power of the Spirit does to this motley crew of disciples who have been so fearful, and perhaps distrustful of one another. Something new is in the air. They now proclaim, as publicly as possible, that a crucified man is the long-awaited Messiah who offers forgiveness even for those who crucified him. The fact that they can be understood by people of many different languages indicates that with the death and resurrection of Jesus and the coming of the Spirit, the failure of communication signaled in Genesis by the tower of Babel has been overcome. On this day in Jerusalem, the people begin to realize what was already implicit in Jesus' own ministry: that the new creation is, in principle, an all-inclusive human family that knows no boundaries of race or language or culture.

See what happens in you as you allow this scene to capture your imagination. If you wish, you can contemplate the picture of the new community drawn in Acts 4:32–37. It may be an idealized picture, but it says something about what the Spirit effected and also of what God wants of the community animated by the Spirit.

The Spirit and the Gentiles

Another contemplation you might want to try is that of chapter 10 of Acts, the story of Peter's conversion to a larger understanding of the community God wants. A pagan, Cornelius, has a vision that tells him to contact Peter and ask him to come from Joppa to Caesarea. In the meantime, Peter, too, has a dream, which tells him not to consider profane the food that God has made clean. As Peter ponders this dream, Cornelius's envoys arrive. Then "the Spirit said to [Peter], 'Look, three men are searching for you. Now get up, go down, and go with them without hesitation; for I have sent them" (10:19–20). Peter goes to the house of Cornelius, and an extraordinary event occurs there:

> While Peter was still speaking, the Holy Spirit fell upon all who heard the word. The circumcised believers who had come with Peter were astounded that the gift of the Holy Spirit had been poured out even on the Gentiles, for they heard them speaking in tongues and extolling God. Then Peter said, "Can anyone withhold the water for baptizing these people who have received the Holy Spirit just as we have?" So he ordered them to be baptized in the name of Jesus Christ. Then they invited him to stay for several days. (10:44–48)

As you contemplate this scene, how are you affected? Do you feel a desire to say, "Yes, that's how it should be, a world where barriers of race, culture, and religion are torn down"? Here a momentous shift in the infant community of Jesus' followers takes place through the outpouring of the Holy Spirit. Gentiles are baptized without having to be circumcised beforehand. The new, all-inclusive community that God desires is gradually being born through the gift of the Spirit.

As I pondered this scene before writing this section, I recalled the preface to the Second Eucharistic Prayer for Masses of Reconciliation that can be used in the Roman Catholic Church. I invite you to pray this prayer with me and to reflect on its meaning:

> Father, all-powerful and ever-living God, we praise and thank you through Jesus Christ our Lord for your presence and action in the world.
>
> In the midst of conflict and division, we know it is you who turn our minds to thoughts of peace. Your Spirit changes our hearts: enemies begin to speak to one another, those who were estranged join hands in friendship, and nations seek the way of peace together.
>
> Your Spirit is at work when understanding puts an end to strife, when hatred is quenched by mercy, and vengeance gives way to forgiveness.
>
> For this we should never cease to thank and praise you.

This prayer speaks of the work of the Spirit in the world. Perhaps you can think of some examples of such work in your family, in your job, in the world. You might, for example, remember a time when—miraculously, it seemed—a long-standing family feud was resolved or two estranged friends shook hands. The Holy Spirit works to bring about what God wants—a world where human beings are friends of God, friends of one another, and friends of the universe that sustains us.

The Work of the Spirit in the Human Community

A personal example of the work of the Spirit may help you bring to mind your own stories. A few years ago, I was on the board of directors for Nativity Prep, a middle school for poor boys sponsored by the New England Jesuits in the inner city of Boston. The boys were African American, Hispanic American, Asian American, and Anglo American. Given the realities of the inner city, they should have been "enemies"—members, perhaps, of rival gangs. But at graduation each year, boy after boy talked of how he loved his peers. One year, on the spur of the moment, I was asked to say something at the end of graduation. With tears in my eyes, I said that what had happened to them in their three years in this school was an example of what God wants for all human beings—namely, that we all become friends. I went on to tell them that in the future, things might not be so rosy, but they should remember that something extraordinary had happened here, and if it happened here, it could happen anywhere, by the grace of God.

What the Spirit did in that school the Spirit does in many places. When we see such community happen, it touches us deeply, because this is what God wants for all of us, and deep in our hearts we know this and want it, too.

The ideal community envisioned by God is one where each person cares for all the others so that no one has to worry about him- or herself. No such community yet exists. Moreover, movements toward a community of this kind often founder after an initial euphoria, and this foundering reinforces the feeling that such a community is a pipe dream. The Spirit, however, wants to move us in this direction, and in our better moments we want to be moved. Take the time to let these movements have their day in you.

In moments of doubt about your community, your church, your country, or the world, which may come often in these difficult times, you may be helped by contemplating a scene from the book of the prophet Ezekiel, who wrote for the Israelite community exiled in Babylon:

> The hand of the LORD came upon me, and he brought me out by the spirit of the LORD and set me down in the middle of a valley; it was full of bones. He led me all around them; there were very many lying in the valley, and they were very dry. He said to me, "Mortal, can these bones live?" I answered, "O Lord GOD, you know." Then he said to me, "Prophesy to these bones, and say to them: O dry bones, hear the

word of the LORD. Thus says the Lord GOD to these bones: I will cause breath to enter you, and you shall live. I will lay sinews on you, and will cause flesh to come upon you, and cover you with skin, and put breath in you, and you shall live; and you shall know that I am the LORD."

So I prophesied as I had been commanded; and as I prophesied, suddenly there was a noise, a rattling, and the bones came together, bone to its bone. I looked, and there were sinews on them, and flesh had come upon them, and skin had covered them; but there was no breath in them. Then he said to me, "Prophesy to the breath, prophesy, mortal, and say to the breath: Thus says the Lord GOD: Come from the four winds, O breath, and breathe upon these slain, that they may live." I prophesied as he commanded me, and the breath came into them, and they lived, and stood on their feet, a vast multitude.

Then he said to me, "Mortal, these bones are the whole house of Israel. They say, 'Our bones are dried up, and our hope is lost; we are cut off completely.' Therefore prophesy, and say to them, Thus says the Lord GOD: I am going to open your graves, and bring you up from your graves, O my people; and I will bring you back to the land of Israel. And you shall know that I am the LORD, when I open your graves, and bring you up from your graves, O my people. I will put my spirit within you, and you shall live, and I will place you on your own soil; then you shall know that I, the LORD, have spoken and will act," says the LORD. (37:1–14)

I hope that the exercises of this chapter are giving you a chance to experience the outpouring of the Spirit on you and those around you. God's dream can seem idealistic in the face of the realities of our world. What we experience in these contemplations is the Holy Spirit working to bring about the new human community that God wants.

A Contemplation to Grow More in Love with God

I end this part of the book devoted to exercises aimed at giving you a chance to experience God's desire for your friendship with an exercise from *The Spiritual Exercises* called the "Contemplation to Attain Love." In this last contemplation, Ignatius makes two preliminary observations that support the point I have been making throughout this book:

First. Love ought to manifest itself more by deeds than by words.

Second. Love consists in a mutual communication between the two persons. That is, the one who loves gives and communicates to the beloved what he or she has, or a part of what one has or can have; and the beloved in return does the same to the lover. Thus, if the one has knowledge, one gives it to the other who does not; and similarly in regard to honors or riches. Each shares with the other. (*The Spiritual Exercises*, n. 230–31)

Here Ignatius is using the analogy of human friendship to speak of the relationship with God. It is extraordinary to think that God wants our gifts just as much as we want God's gifts. God has created us for such mutuality. "Each shares with the other," Ignatius writes.

Ignatius then proposes some points for reflection so that we can experience God's prolific generosity and realize that God wants, but does not demand, our generosity, as a token of friendship. In the points Ignatius proposes, he hopes that we will "contemplate"—that is, see, touch, and sense—what God is doing in ongoing creation. The purpose of this contemplation is to draw out of us a corresponding love for God, a desire to give God all that we are, just as God has given us all that God is. In what follows, I suggest that you ask God's Spirit to help you taste God's presence in all of creation.

In the first of the four points, we are encouraged to remember all the gifts we have received: "I will ponder with deep affection how much God our Lord has done for me, and how much he has given me of what he possesses, and consequently how he, the same Lord, desires to give me even his very self, in accordance with his divine design" (*The Spiritual Exercises*, n. 234). Other translations of this last phrase make it a poignant statement: "It is the Lord's wish, as far as he is able, to give me himself."

God wants to give me as much of Godself as is possible. That is an amazing statement. In response, I am encouraged to offer God all of myself: my liberty, my memory, my intelligence, my understanding, my entire will—"all that I have and possess." The mutuality is moving toward fullness. Of course, we approach this ideal only by a circuitous route that includes much resistance. Developing an intimate friendship with God is a lifetime proposition. One deep experience of this "Contemplation to Attain Love" does not guarantee that we will remain in close union with God. God is infinitely patient with our fumbling and resistance to the gift of friendship; we need to imitate God in patience.

In the other points, Ignatius has us consider how God dwells in everything, how God labors for us in all of creation, and how all good things and gifts come from God. If you come to experience the world in this way, then you are a contemplative in action—that is, one who finds God in all things. This Ignatian notion can be understood as analogous to the kind of friendship that develops over a long time between two people. They are aware of each other even when they are apart or not engaging directly with each other. Although they may not be talking, at some deep level they are in touch with each other. Ignatius's contemplative in action has such a relationship with God. Engaging closely with God over time, we allow the Spirit to transform us into people who are more like the images of God we are created to be—that is, more like Jesus, who was clearly a contemplative in action.

The aim of these exercises is to help you develop a close friendship with the triune God. You can return to the exercises throughout your life insofar as they continue to be helpful. Of course, you and God will find many other ways to grow in friendship and to cooperate more fully in God's creative project. If you continue to grow in this friendship, you will discover how inventive God is, and how inventive you are. The friendship with God is indeed a friendship like no other, since God is Mystery itself. We turn now to questions for prayer and reflection that arise when we take seriously the notion that God wants our friendship.

PART II

Understanding Ourselves and God

» 6

How Could God Want My Friendship?

Some of you may be wondering whether what you have read and experienced thus far in this book is too good to be true. You might be thinking, *How could God have time for the likes of me? After all, I'm nobody, except perhaps to my family and friends. It seems rash to think that God wants me to be a friend. I've failed miserably to live up to what God expects of me. I'm not worthy of God's friendship.*

If these thoughts have occurred to you, read on. If not, you can skip to the next chapter, where I look at another objection to the ideas explored in part 1.

Our Insignificance and God's Desire
One persistent source of resistance to God's desire for friendship is the notion that I am too insignificant to be of concern to God—except, of course, when I fail to live

up to God's expectations. Then I am the object of God's anger. Even if I can be convinced that God does care for some people, I find it much harder to believe that God cares for me. As a result, I remain at a distance from God and consider myself justified, perhaps even virtuous, in maintaining that distance.

Psalm 8 expresses this objection rather pointedly:

> When I look at your heavens, the work of your
>   fingers,
>   the moon and the stars that you have established;
> what are human beings that you are mindful of
>   them,
>   mortals that you care for them?
>   (8:3–4)

The psalmist speaks for the people of his day and for all of us. We, who have a modern knowledge of the vastness of the universe in both space and time, can affirm these words with even more confidence. But the psalmist does not stop with the objection. He goes on to speak of what God wants:

> Yet you have made them a little lower than God,
>   and crowned them with glory and honor.
> You have given them dominion over the works of
>   your hands;
>   you have put all things under their feet,

all sheep and oxen,
    and also the beasts of the field,
the birds of the air, and the fish of the sea,
    whatever passes along the paths of the seas.

O LORD, our Sovereign,
    how majestic is your name in all the earth!
        (8:5–9)

The psalmist, aware of how insignificant we human beings are in the vast scheme of creation, expresses awe that God should want us as cooperators in the creative enterprise. And then, it seems, he submits to God's desire. I take the psalmist's proclamation that God gives human beings "dominion over the works of your hands" as a reference to the creation story of Genesis, which we have already explored as an invitation to friendship with God. At the end of the psalm, the psalmist praises God's majesty and generosity.

The issue is not our insignificance, which is true enough, but what God desires in creating us. The Pulitzer Prize–winning poet Franz Wright expresses this very well in the following lines from "Preparations":

While there is time

I call to mind Your constant unrequited
and preemptive forgiveness.

And remember You are not
and never were the object
of my thought,
my prayer,
my words

> but rather *I*
> *was the object of Yours!*

And I think I'm beginning to learn finally
what everything has been trying to teach me
just recently
again, and
for the past fifty years of forever:
total love for You—the mysterious gift of my life—
truly felt at each instant
and every day
of deepest recollection,
grace-filled apprehension, it *would*
dispel all fear, as well
as the love that requires a response—
from others, other
ghosts (or
even
You!)

The biggest obstacle to a true relationship with God is our belief that the relationship depends, ultimately, on us. This is the wisdom that Wright, no doubt after much soul searching, comes to in his poem. If God wants my friendship, it doesn't matter how insignificant I feel.

In the poem, I also detect a reference to the first letter of John, in which he says:

> God is love, and those who abide in love abide in God, and God abides in them. Love has been perfected among us in this: that we may have boldness on the day of judgment, because as he is, so are we in this world. There is no fear in love, but perfect love casts out fear; for fear has to do with punishment, and whoever fears has not reached perfection in love. We love because he first loved us. (4:16–19)

John writes that "perfect love casts out fear." Perhaps Wright is referring indirectly to this statement when he writes that he is finally beginning to understand that total love for God—"the mysterious gift of my life"—"*would /* dispel all fear," even the fear that God's love depends on our response. God's love for us does not depend on us and what we do. God loves us first, and without any impetus on our part.

God's love creates us for no other reason than God's love. So God's offer of friendship does not depend on our significance, but solely on God's desire for us.

Our Sinfulness and God's Desire

We may also be hung up in our acceptance of God's offer of friendship by our feelings of sinful unworthiness. In chapter 3, we engaged in exercises to help us experience God's forgiveness. The fruit of those exercises, I hope, was the realization that divine love does not change with our failure to live up to God's hopes and dreams for us. But even though we experience God's forgiveness, we may still cling to our unsavory past and, because of this, have doubts about being called to friendship with God. Here again, we make God's desire dependent on us.

While we might believe that we are only being humble in acknowledging the obvious truth that we are unworthy of God's friendship, our egocentricity is actually revealed in this belief. With it, we make ourselves the arbiter of what God wants. In John's Gospel, Jesus says, "For God so loved the world that he gave his only Son, so that everyone who believes in him may not perish but may have eternal life" (3:16). Later in the Gospel, Jesus defines eternal life: "That they may know you, the only true God, and Jesus Christ whom you have sent" (17:3). As we noted earlier, the word *know* here refers to heart knowledge. God deliberately gives the Son to a sinful world—indeed, to a world that would kill the Son. If God's love and offer of friendship did not end with the crucifixion of Jesus, then it will never end.

At the thirty-second General Congregation of the Society of Jesus, in 1974–75, the delegates asked, "What is it to be a Jesuit today?" The response was "It is to know that one is a sinner, yet called to be a companion of Jesus as Ignatius was." In this short sentence, the Jesuits expressed a truth that applies to everyone. We are all sinners and are all called to be friends of God.

I urge you to ask God to purge from your heart the vestiges of fear that produce feelings of insignificance and unworthiness. You do God no favor by thinking stingily or meanly about the person who is the apple of God's eye— you. In *The Impact of God*, the Carmelite Iain Matthew writes very movingly of the spirituality of St. John of the Cross, the sixteenth-century Spanish Carmelite mystic. At one point, Matthew notes John's insistence on faith rather than evidence for the development of the relationship with God. Matthew goes on: "The danger envisaged is not so much that we shall trust in the wrong thing, but that we shall stop trusting at all; that, while we may never say it in so many words, we shall cease to believe that we are a factor in God's life."

A factor in God's life! That is how much God values each one of us, according to one of the great mystics and saints of Christianity.

» 7

Isn't This a Self-Centered Spirituality?

In the early 1970s, when Jesuits began to rediscover the
ministry of spiritual direction and the method of giving
the Spiritual Exercises to individuals, a tension developed
between Jesuits involved in social action for a just world and
those engaged in spiritual direction. To the social activists,
the work of spiritual direction involved too much navel-
gazing at a time when the structures of our world fostered
social injustice on a massive scale. To those in the ministry
of spiritual direction, on the other hand, social action that
wasn't grounded in a strong personal relationship with God
risked becoming destructive.

The question raised by the social activists may have
occurred to you as you prayed and reflected on the ideas
explored thus far. Is my stress on friendship with God promot-
ing an inward-looking, self-centered spirituality that ignores

the larger issues faced by our world? To address this objection, I want to introduce a new analogy into our discussion. We have been looking at human friendship as an analogy for the friendship we are called to with God. Now I want to look at the relationship between adult children and their parents, which, as I will show, is also a friendship, and one that can give us clues about how we are to live in this world as friends of God.

The Image of God as Parent

We are often taught to see God as a parent. Jesus, who called God "Abba" ("dear Father"), said to his followers, "Pray then in this way: / Our Father in heaven" (Matthew 6:9), telling us that we have a similar relationship with God. Many people have been heartened by this image of God as a father or mother and have, through its use, come to a love of God that was impossible when God seemed more forbidding. Usually, however, when preachers and teachers speak of God as Father or Mother, they invoke images of a parent with a child: "God holds us as a mother holds an infant in her arms." "God wants to console and comfort us as a parent cuddles a child." "God welcomes sinners back as a father or mother welcomes a wayward child." "God punishes us the way a good parent does for our good." At times, of course, such images are quite appropriate for an adult. But how does a forty-five-year-old parent of young children who also works a full-time job react to such images? How do you react to them?

I propose that the relationship between an adult child and his or her parent is a better image of the relationship God wants with us as adults. Let's reflect for a moment on adult relationships with parents. As we mature into adulthood, we become more like peers of our parents. Of course, they are always our parents, always "Mom" or "Dad," and we continue to bestow upon them a kind of reverence because they gave us life and raised us. But we no longer expect to be held in their arms, except in extreme circumstances. Nor do we expect them to tell us what to do with our lives, although some parents never seem to lose the desire to tell their children what to do. Rather, we become more like equals as we take on the same adult roles they have had. Now that we know what adulthood entails, we become more sympathetic to them. We realize what they went through to earn a living and rear us through childhood, and especially through our teen years. We may even find that we treat them as good friends, confiding in them without expecting them to shoulder the burdens we know we alone have to carry.

I believe that this kind of relationship between an adult child and his or her parents is more like what God wants with us as we grow into adulthood. In addition, I sense that more adults will find religious preaching and teaching intriguing, challenging, and even exciting if those of us who engage in these ministries begin to use such imagery when speaking of our relationship with God. How do you react to this idea?

God's Family Business

Now that we have established that the relationship between an adult child and his or her parent is a fitting analogy for the relationship God wants with us, we can address the objection to this being a self-centered spirituality. The answer lies in the collaboration in the family business that we are called to as friends of God. God's family business is discipleship. This is not a business we can run on our own. It involves the community of all of God's friends working together to bring about a more just and harmonious world.

In our adult relationships with our parents, we are sometimes called or drawn to work with them. Our parents may own a business that we join as adults, or we may work the same trade or in the same industry and decide to collaborate on a project or business venture. In the course of our work together on a common task, we grow in mutuality, in camaraderie, and in friendship.

In chapter 2, we saw this same type of collaboration in the second creation story in Genesis. God and human beings engage in the work of developing the garden, our planet, together. They cultivate the garden together, and after a day of work, at the time of the evening breeze, God comes to meet them for a chat about the day. This image is one of an adult friendship between God and human beings that includes shared work and shared relaxation.

The story of creation shows that God's family business is not in the church, but the world. It is not reserved just for religious people, nor is it the work of individuals working independently. The family business into which we are invited as adult friends of God entails a community working together. As noted in chapter 2, we are all co-laborers in God's work of creation. The work cannot be accomplished without the cooperation of each one of us.

How do you react to this meditation? Does it address your objection?

» 8

Where Does Salvation Figure In to Friendship with God?

On New Year's Day 2006, I was praying with the liturgical readings of the day, the first of which was Numbers 6:22–27:

> The LORD spoke to Moses, saying: Speak to Aaron and his sons, saying, Thus you shall bless the Israelites: You shall say to them,
>
> > The LORD bless you and keep you;
> > the LORD make his face to shine upon you, and be gracious to you;
> > the LORD lift up his countenance upon you, and give you peace.

> So they shall put my name on the Israelites, and I will
> bless them.

The Gospel text for the day was Luke 2:16–21, which includes the circumcision and naming of Jesus—a name that, in Hebrew, means "God saves." One of the questions that popped into my mind was, how does God save through offering friendship?

You might also be wondering what friendship with God has to do with our need for salvation, a central theme of Judeo-Christian religion. In this meditation, I will show that we are saved by gracefully accepting God's offer of friendship.

Naming and Friendship

I invite you to look more carefully at the blessing God gave to Moses in chapter 6 of Numbers, as I did that New Year's Day. Three times God uses the name he gave to Moses: it is spelled YHWH in the Hebrew Bible and is here translated as "Lord." This is the name that pious Jews do not say aloud, but that many Christians often sing or say—Yahweh.

The Israelites avoided expressing the full name of God because in those times naming someone meant being on intimate terms with the person named, and in some sense having control over that person. In Genesis, God names Adam and Eve, and they in turn name the other creatures. The "stronger" names the "weaker," as it were. Yet God lets Moses know the name YHWH, in some way putting a human being on a par with God.

Think about this issue of naming for a moment. In some cultures, such as the German and the French, the use of a person's first name is restricted to members of the person's family and intimate friends. Until you are given permission to use a person's first name, you use a formal "you" when speaking to him or her. (I believe that these distinctions are now disappearing, at least in Germany.) If you want to show your desire for a closer friendship with another person, you ask him to use your first name and hope that he will reciprocate. You take a risk by asking, because the person may reject your request.

In the United States, the use of nicknames often indicates a move to a closer friendship and to deeper trust. Usually we give nicknames to those we like, and a nickname often reflects a playful sense of humor between two friends. When you give someone a nickname, you take a risk that the other might be offended.

In the Bible, we find some instances of such a shift in relationship between human beings and God. In chapter 2, we noted that God changed the names of Abram and Sarai to Abraham and Sarah, indicating a deepening of their friendship. Jesus seems to have used nicknames to indicate a closer friendship with others. For example, he renames Simon Cephas in Aramaic, or Petra in Greek, which means "Rock." The New Testament scholar Daniel Harrington, SJ, suggests that "Peter/Cephas may not have been a proper name but rather a nickname, which perhaps had some connection with Peter's personal characteristics ('Rocky')." It also indicates a friendly sense of humor on Jesus' part, which we may see again in Jesus' naming of the brothers James and John as "Sons of Thunder." Did Zebedee, the father of James and John, react thunderously to the sudden loss of both of his sons from the family fishing business?

These examples show that naming is connected with the offer of friendship and involves some vulnerability. The vulnerability arises, in the first place, from the fact that the other may refuse the name, and thus the offer of friendship. But the vulnerability does not end there. In fact, it increases in direct proportion to the closeness of the friendship. The closer I am with you in friendship, the more devastated you will be if I betray it. This direct relationship between closeness and vulnerability may explain how betrayal of the closest relationships often leads to the bitterest enmity.

God's Vulnerability and Our Salvation

On that New Year's Day, reading about the naming of Jesus opened up a new vista for me. In Jesus, God saves by becoming so vulnerable that we are able to kill him in a vile and humiliating way. The crucifixion and resurrection of Jesus assure us that God's offer of friendship will never be withdrawn, no matter what we do. If the cross did not result in a withdrawal of the offer, then nothing we do will lead to a change of heart in God.

We can, however, refuse the offer. Friendship is a mutual relationship, and one has to accept the offer; one cannot be coerced or tricked into it. And the final refusal by any human being of God's offer of friendship breaks God's heart. Still, God does not turn away in anger and rage from such a person. God lives eternally with a broken heart. That's how vulnerable God wants to be.

If God wants friendship with all human beings, then our salvation consists in accepting this offer of friendship. In other words, from the beginning of human existence on earth, God's plan for the world has entailed human acceptance of God's friendship. We turned away from this friendship and lost our way. We were in need of salvation from our folly. God's answer was to renew the offer of friendship and to send the Son to share our lot and show us how to live as friends of God. Thus, the saving of the world comes about heart by heart, as it were. God offers friendship to each human being not only as a path to his or her salvation but also as a means to the salvation of the world. From the moment we become conscious of being responsible human beings, each of us is faced with a choice: to be the human being God creates us to be—God's friend and thus part of God's solution for our world—or to be part of the problem that needs fixing or conversion.

Our Vulnerability as a Response to God's Vulnerability

It is clear that the friendship God offers cannot be had in isolation from other human beings. Just as human friendship entails becoming friends of my friend's friends and family, so, too, becoming a friend of God involves accepting God's other friends, at least in principle. Mind you, God's other friends are potentially all the people on the planet. So my joy, my fulfillment, my salvation consists in opening myself to friendship with God and with every man, woman, and child ever created. At the least, I must be open to conversation with God about having such a large heart.

We are created in the image and likeness of God, and God has shown that it is the divine nature to be vulnerable to friendship. If we are to image God, we can do so only by allowing ourselves to become vulnerable as God is vulnerable. By accepting God's offer of friendship, we are drawn into vulnerability in friendship with all of God's friends and potential friends. This drawing is the work of the Holy Spirit dwelling in our hearts.

What the Name YHWH Reveals about God

It might help to look at the privileged moment of God's self-revelation in the Hebrew Bible, the revelation to Moses at the burning bush. God has just expressed his compassion for the suffering Israelites and told Moses to go bring them out of Egypt.

But Moses said to God, "If I come to the Israelites and say to them, 'The God of your ancestors has sent me to you,' and they ask me, 'What is his name?' what shall I say to them?" God said to Moses, "I AM WHO I AM." He said further, "Thus you shall say to the Israelites, 'I AM has sent me to you.'" God also said to Moses, "Thus you shall say to the Israelites, 'The LORD, the God of your ancestors, the God of Abraham, the God of Isaac, and the God of Jacob, has sent me to you':

> This is my name forever,
> and this my title for all generations."
> (Exodus 3:13–15)

Most Western philosophers and theologians have tended to understand the words "I am who I am" in philosophical terms. The name is interpreted to mean that God is the supreme being, being itself. But the name is notoriously difficult to translate. The New Revised Standard Version of the Bible, which always translates *YHWH* as "LORD," says in a footnote that it could mean "I am what I am" or "I will be what I will be."

In *A Theology of Compassion*, the English theologian Oliver Davies notes that the rabbinic tradition has a different take on this revelation. In this tradition, the name revealed, YHWH, speaks of God's compassion for the world, a compassion that will only be fully revealed over time. The Hebrew word for compassion (*raham*) is associated with the word for womb and can be translated as "womb love," a compassion that is deeply felt and leads the one who has it to risk him- or herself for another.

Davies quotes Rabbi Abba bar Mammel, who said:

> God said to Moses: I am called according to my acts. At times I am called El Shaddai, Seba'ot, Elohim and Yahweh. When I judge creatures, I am called Elohim; when I forgive sins, I am called El Shaddai; when I wage war against the wicked, I am called Seba'ot, and when I show compassion for my world, I am called Yahweh.

Davies believes that we should take seriously this understanding of God's self-revelation for the sake of the world to which God shows compassion. God, in whose image we are created, takes risks for the sake of the world and invites us to do the same.

Christians believe that God shows compassion in the most telling way in Jesus of Nazareth. God's compassion for the world leads God to risk taking on human flesh and being killed for doing so. In the contemplation on the Incarnation in *The Spiritual Exercises*, Ignatius of Loyola asks us to imagine the Trinity looking down on the world and seeing "all the peoples in such great blindness, and how they are dying and going down to hell" and then saying, "Let us work the redemption of the human race" (nn. 106, 107). In spite of what we read about God's blazing anger at sinful Israel in many passages of the Bible, God, in compassion for us, risks being rejected and killed as one of us.

Here is the God in whose image we are created. When Jesus says that we are to be perfect as our heavenly Father is perfect (Matthew 5:48), he means that we are to be compassionate.

To be compassionate means to feel so profoundly for others in trouble or pain that we will put ourselves at risk to help them. That's how God's compassion works. We live in this world as God's images insofar as we show compassion for others in the way God shows compassion. Since God is the creator of all human beings and, indeed, of all of creation, we cannot limit our compassion to our own family, tribe, or nation.

Iain Matthew writes of a poem of John of the Cross that it

sings of a God who *is* community. Father, Son, in Spirit: living water in infinite exchange. And that God is community with a *maximum* immigration policy. . . . Theirs is a love secure enough to let them be vulnerable. So John knows a living water that just loves to overflow so as to gather all else in its flow.

What a lovely image: "a maximum immigration policy." No one is excluded from this vulnerable offer.

Another Objection

Now another objection may come to the fore: I am too weak and sinful to follow the way of Jesus. That kind of following is only for the saints and heroes of our world, not for the likes of me. After all, Jesus was divine. How can I imitate him?

Once, I gave some talks on the human Jesus to seminarians in New Orleans. In the first talk, I focused on how difficult it is for us to take seriously that Jesus was a real human being who had to be toilet trained, to learn language, to work out his vocation, and to discern the will of God, just as we do. I then said that we cannot do justice to our faith in his humanity unless we are willing to predicate such human learning of him. At the beginning of the second talk, one seminarian was brave enough to make the following confession before his fellow seminarians and the faculty: "I realize why I don't take seriously that Jesus was a human being like me. If I do, I will have to imitate him."

How can we believe that Jesus is human as we are, sin the lone exception? He is human enough to be imitated by us.

Since the dawn of creation, human beings have been called to be images of God. In a way, God had to show us how to do it by becoming one of us. In Jesus, God showed us compassion, and we have no excuses for not imitating Jesus in this. We can do it because God creates us for this role, gives us the Spirit to move our hearts and minds to such compassion, and gives us Jesus to show us the way: "I am the way, and the truth, and the life" (John 14:6).

But often when our hearts and minds are moved to compassion, we turn away, because we don't want to take the risk. The future of our world, however, depends on our willingness to live as the human beings God has created us to be. Being human means allowing our hearts to be touched by the plight of our fellow humans and taking action for the sake of the other.

According to Matthew 25, we will be judged by how well we show compassion for those in need:

> Then the righteous will answer him, "Lord, when was it that we saw you hungry and gave you food, or thirsty and gave you something to drink? And when was it that we saw you a stranger and welcomed you, or naked and gave you clothing? And when was it that we saw you sick or in prison and visited you?" And the king will answer them, "Truly I tell you, just as you did it to one of the least of these who are members of my family, you did it to me." (25:37–40)

Clearly Jesus believes that it is possible for us to show compassion, so possible that we are culpable if we do not. The future of our planet depends on us—on how we live as the image and likeness of God.

Mary, the Mother of Jesus, as Model

In a powerful poem, "Annunciation," Denise Levertov portrays Mary's courage as the kind of courage God hopes to find in all of us. But, perhaps inadvertently, she also portrays God's vulnerability. I invite you to let this poem reverberate within you.

We know the scene: the room, variously furnished,
almost always a lectern, a book; always
the tall lily.
     Arrived on solemn grandeur of great wings,
the angelic ambassador, standing or hovering,
whom she acknowledges, a guest.

But we are told of meek obedience. No one
     mentions
courage.
     The engendering Spirit
did not enter her without consent.
          God waited.

She was free
to accept or to refuse, choice
integral to humanness.

Aren't there annunciations
of one sort or another
in most lives?

      Some unwillingly
undertake great destinies,
enact them in sullen pride,
uncomprehending.

    More often
those moments

  when roads of light and storm

  open from darkness in a man or woman,
are turned away from
in dread, in a wave of weakness, in despair
and with relief.
Ordinary lives continue.

        God does not smite them.
But the gates close, the pathway vanishes.

She had been a child who played, ate, slept
like any other child—but unlike others,
wept only for pity, laughed
in joy not triumph.
Compassion and intelligence
fused in her, indivisible.

Called to a destiny more momentous
than any in all of Time,
she did not quail,
            only asked
a simple, 'How can this be?'
and gravely, courteously,
took to heart the angel's reply,
perceiving instantly
the astounding ministry she was offered:

to bear in her womb
Infinite weight and lightness; to carry
in hidden, finite inwardness,
nine months of Eternity; to contain
in slender vase of being,
the sum of power—
in narrow flesh,
the sum of light.
            Then bring to birth,
push out into air, a Man-child
needing, like any other,
milk and love—

but who was God.

As God did with Mary, God waits for each one of
us to respond to the offer of friendship. In that waiting,

God is vulnerable. If Mary had refused the invitation, the Messiah would not have been Jesus of Nazareth. The historical reality of our redemption needed Mary's acceptance. Though we have a different destiny than Mary in God's plan, God extends the same offer of friendship, and the historical reality of the future of the world, in some small fashion, depends on our response to God's vulnerability.

» 9

Does Friendship Lead to Compassion for God?

We feel compassion for our friends and are moved to take risks to help them. But have you ever felt compassion for God? Perhaps the reason we don't often do so is that we do not sense the mutuality in our friendship with God.

For the past few years, I have begun each period of prayer by asking to be aware of God's presence. Many times, of course, I am quite distracted, but when grace works, I become aware of God creating and sustaining the whole world and, at the same time, attending to me. Sometimes I have also realized that God is present in the same way to hurricane and earthquake victims, to refugees driven from their homes by war and terror, and to people mourning almost unendurable losses. I have been deeply moved with sympathy for these many suffering people. I have wondered, "If I can feel sympathy for these people from reading about their plight or seeing it on television, what must God's reactions be?"

God is, after all, not reading or hearing about the suffering of his people, but right there with them, sustaining them along with the whole universe. I believe that my best reactions are only pale reflections of God's reactions. Perhaps, indeed, God is calling me to an adult friendship in which there is a mutuality of compassion. Let's reflect together on this possibility.

What God Witnesses and Sustains

God creates and sustains all that exists, including the sick and evil people who do incalculable harm to their fellow human beings. A few days after Christmas, Christians celebrate the Feast of the Holy Innocents. You may recall the story from the Gospel of Matthew: Herod the Great, in a fit of anger and desperation, orders the killing of all baby boys two years old or younger in the environs of Bethlehem. He wants to ensure the death of the "king of the Jews" sought by the Magi. Of course, we do not know for sure whether this story precisely reflects historical fact, although it fits with what is known of the character of Herod. It seems he did not shrink from killing his own sons when he thought that they might be a threat to his rule. So it is possible that he could have done this horrible deed if he heard that a new king had been born in Bethlehem. Things like this still happen all the time in our world. Innocent children are maimed and killed, sometimes for political reasons.

A year ago when I was contemplating this scene of the murder of the Holy Innocents, I thought that God seemed to suffer the unintended consequence of the birth of Jesus: the killing of the innocent babies. I could imagine God weeping like Rachel "for her children" (Matthew 2:18).

Perhaps you will see what I mean by feeling compassion for God by reading the heartbreaking experience of Rebecca Ann Parker as told in *Proverbs of Ashes*. She was raped when she was four years old by a neighbor, Frank. As a result, she had to undergo many years of therapy and had a number of difficult relationships with men. At one point, her therapist told her that they would have to find some way "to go back into that bedroom at Frank's house so that the child left for dead was not left alone in Frank's house." Parker was terrified and did not want to do this, but she finally concluded that she must: "As long as part of me was left there, in Frank's house, I wasn't going to be whole. I was settling for a piece of me to be abandoned eternally to the abuser." During a session with her therapist, she was able to return to that place of horror. She later wrote about the experience in an e-mail to her coauthor:

> When I was raped as a child, there was a moment that
> I have been able to remember in which I was quite

sure I was going to die—and perhaps I was, in fact, close to being killed.

I was being orally raped. I couldn't breathe. I was just a small child! Four years old. And the weight of the man on top of me was crushing. In that moment I knew that there was a Presence with me that was "stronger" than the rapist and that could encompass my terror. This Presence had a quality of unbounded compassion for me and unbreakable connection to me, an encompassing embrace of me and, for that matter, of the man raping me. I understood that if I died, I would somehow still be with this Presence, this Presence would "take me up," this Presence was "greater than" death, and "greater than" the power of the man who was raping me.

This Presence could not stop the man from killing me, if he chose to. And, at the same time, it *could* stop him. Because, I knew, if he noticed [the Presence] he *would* be stopped. He would not be able to continue. You couldn't. It was clear to me. You *couldn't* be aware of this Presence and do what the man was doing to me. He only could do it by not noticing, not knowing. So, this Presence *did* have the power to save me from death and there is a way in which I believe it did. The man did stop short of killing me, and I think it was because some part of him could not ultimately deny the knowledge that he was raping God. Not that I was God, obviously, but that the Presence was there and in raping me he was going against the Presence.

When I sense God's presence to such horrors, I am often brought to tears. It's heartbreaking to think of God, the loving, compassionate One, sustaining Frank during such a deed. Do you feel something like compassion for God as you imagine this scene?

What must it be like for God to be present to such events! If we can be moved to compassion, how much more must God be moved, who not only hears about what has happened but is also present and sustaining the perpetrators of such horrors!

St. Teresa of Ávila, the sixteenth-century Spanish Carmelite reformer and mystic, described God as an immense and beautiful palace in which everything that exists dwells. She wrote, "It is the most dreadful thing in the world that God our Creator should suffer so many misdeeds to be committed by His creatures within Himself." Her reflections give us something to ponder as we read the newspaper and watch the news on television. Perhaps if we reflect on God's sustaining presence to all the horrors of our world, we will be sympathetic to, even compassionate toward, God and thus more of an adult friend.

A Mutuality of Compassion

Once, a woman who is a chaplain in an acute care unit of a large hospital spoke to me of what she had experienced in a twenty-four-hour period. Among a number of incidents that day, she was called to comfort a mother who had just delivered dead twins, to minister to a mother whose newborn baby was dying because of the mother's drug use, and to bless a baby whose brain was dead because of a severe shaking, probably by the mother. As she prepared for this last meeting, she prayed for the grace to do what God wanted and that her anger at the mother would not get in the way. When the chaplain got to the room, the mother broke down in her arms, and all the chaplain could do was hold her with compassion.

After this heart-wrenching day, the chaplain sought comfort from God. She wanted God to hold her and caress her the way a mother might hold a child in great pain. When she did not get that comfort, she got angry with God.

As I listened to her story, I became aware of how God was present as the mother shook her baby. God was also present at the other terrible situations that led to this chaplain's day, as well as at innumerable others throughout the world. After talking with the chaplain for some time about her reactions and frustration, I wondered aloud if she was being called to a new step in her relationship with God, to a mutuality of compassion. She then remembered hearing God say recently, "We have to learn to trust one another more." Perhaps, indeed, God was asking her for mutuality in compassion. The following weeks seemed to confirm this idea as she continued to pray.

I have come to believe that friendship with God can lead us to have compassion for God. I have, of course, wondered whether I was being irreverent or presumptuous, and I have asked God to let me know if I was on the wrong track. So far, I have not experienced any response that would lead me to change my belief. Indeed, I sense that God is pleased that I share the burden. Moreover, I have found myself growing in the ability to listen to stories of horror with compassion. It is not easy to listen to such stories, but I find myself consoled and grateful that I am more able to do so. I wonder whether God is hoping for more and more adult friends who are willing to share God's own pain and thus grow in the ability to listen with compassion to others.

In chapter 5, I provided some exercises to help lead you to compassion for Jesus as he died on the cross. If you were able to engage in those exercises, you have already experienced compassion for the Son of God. You might now also feel compassion for the God who had to sustain the world as this horror was unfolding.

to stop people from committing evil? And how could God allow natural disasters and human evils—such as the tsunamis of December 2004, Hurricane Katrina, the murder of children, and so on—that devastate so many lives? The people who suffer these disasters and evils might well ask what good God's friendship is if it does not save them from such horrors. How can we come to terms with evil in a world created by a compassionate God who wants our friendship?

Why Doesn't God Intervene?

In some ways, a response to the first question can be found in the quotation from Rebecca Ann Parker that we pondered in the last chapter. God cannot coerce human beings to live as images of God. We have freedom and can refuse to live up to our best ideals and God's hopes. As Parker notes, her abuser could not have continued doing what he was doing if he allowed himself to become aware of the Presence. It is our refusal to pay attention to the God-inspired movements of our hearts that allows us to do such evil things to others.

All of us, if we are honest, know that we have done or said hurtful things to others even though we had some qualms about these actions before we did them. We know what it means not to pay attention to the Presence. We can only thank God that we were not faced with the kind of powerful impulses Frank must have had, for we do not know whether we would have paid attention to the Presence either. We can blame the Nazis for the Shoah, but I have to admit that I feel blessed that I was not tested as many Germans were by the propaganda of their government and by fear of the consequences of paying attention to the voice of the Holy Spirit, God's presence in our hearts. "There but for the grace of God go I" is a frequent prayer I make when I read the newspaper or listen to the news. We are all capable of sin.

As we reflected in the last few chapters, God's dream of a world where "they will not hurt or destroy on all my holy mountain" (Isaiah 11:9) cannot come about without the cooperation of all of us, and all of us fall short of God's hopes and expectations. In creating human beings with free will and calling them into friendship, God becomes vulnerable to our weaknesses and fears.

So why doesn't God wipe out the evildoers? Jesus' answer to this question comes in the parable of the weeds among the wheat:

> The kingdom of heaven may be compared to someone who sowed good seed in his field; but while everybody was asleep, an enemy came and sowed weeds among the wheat, and then went away. So when the plants came up and bore grain, then the weeds appeared as well. And the slaves of the householder came and said to him, "Master, did you not sow good seed in your field? Where, then, did these weeds come from?" He answered, "An enemy has done this." The slaves said to him, "Then do you want us to go and gather them?"

> But he replied, "No; for in gathering the weeds you
> would uproot the wheat along with them. Let both of
> them grow together until the harvest; and at harvest
> time I will tell the reapers, Collect the weeds first and
> bind them in bundles to be burned, but gather the
> wheat into my barn." (Matthew 13:24–30)

I don't know about you, but this parable makes me sigh
with relief, because I have often enough been a weed among
the wheat. It is also true, from what we know about the
interconnectedness of everything in the universe, that the
annihilation of anything could mean the annihilation of
everything. Again, I am relieved that God has not given up
on our world in spite of the weeds that we have all been and
sown. What are your reactions?

God's Friendship and Natural Disasters

The second question—why the all-good and all-powerful God
creates a world where natural disasters cause havoc in the lives
of so many people—is the more vexing one. It has bedeviled
humankind perhaps since the dawn of consciousness. I have
not been satisfied with any of the answers I have heard over
the years. Perhaps the only satisfying answer is the one each of
us receives from God when we lament such disasters.

Job seemed satisfied by the response he received from
God after crying out over his misfortunes. In the book of Job,
God responds to Job's complaining with a series of questions.

God tells Job that Job is not God and that only God can know the ultimate mystery of all things. When God has delivered his questions, Job responds:

> I know that you can do all things,
>> and that no purpose of yours can be thwarted. . . .
> Therefore I have uttered what I did not understand,
>> things too wonderful for me, which I did not
>>> know. . . .
> I had heard of you by the hearing of the ear,
>> but now my eye sees you;
> therefore I despise myself,
>> and repent in dust and ashes.
>> (42:2–6)

God's response does not explain the misfortunes that befell Job, and the questions God puts to Job are not an answer to life's catastrophes. They just point to the mystery of the universe God has created. Job's response can seem to be abject and self-abusive. But we can also read his reply more generously as a statement of fact of one who has encountered God. When we encounter God, we know that we are not God and that we exist only because God wants us to exist. In that sense, I can "despise" myself for not having realized the true state of things.

Was Job wrong to want a response from God? God's questions seem to show anger that Job dared to complain and demand a hearing before God. Yet immediately after Job's response, God says to Eliphaz, one of Job's friends who had tried to defend God's ways and shut Job up: "My wrath is kindled against you and against your two friends; for you have not spoken of me what is right, as my servant Job has" (42:7). I take it that Job is being commended for wanting to continue the conversation with God and for refusing to blame himself for what had befallen him.

Job's friends tried to use the usual theological and philosophical explanations for catastrophes, but Job would have none of it. He refused the just-world hypothesis, which lays the blame for disasters on the backs of those who suffer them. Of a woman who was raped, for example, one hears statements such as "She must have been asking for it" or "Why was she out at night without someone to protect her?" Of the victims of hurricanes, one hears "Why did they live so close to the shore?" Job could not accept the arguments of his friends, who seem to have been operating with this hypothesis. He can come across as petulant and angry, but what seems to have pleased God is that Job would not accept false answers and wanted to speak directly to God. Job wanted to continue the friendship, to use the terms of this book.

In Iain Matthew's book on St. John of the Cross, Matthew comments on these passages from the book of Job:

[Job's final response] is the freedom of being able to stand at the back of the temple and say, because now any other statement would be an irrelevance, "God, be merciful to me, a sinner" [Luke 18:13]. It means not cringing submission, but the knowledge that I am part of something bigger than I had ever realized. It brings that mixture of awe, excitement and shame I feel when the one I had been instructing turns out to be a genius. It is knowledge of God which, John says, leads one to treat him with new "respect" and "courtesy."

The book of Job, it seems, was written to address the question of why bad things happen to good people. Ultimately, there is no answer except that God has created this universe as it is, and God is still interested in having friendship with us human beings even when we rage against the misfortunes that so often befall us by no fault of our own. What is your reaction?

I don't have an answer to the question of why there is so much evil and pain in this world. All I can do is encourage you to speak directly to God if you have questions about God's ways, as one friend to another, even if anger is the only emotion you can voice. The book of Job, I believe, encourages such honest relating with one's friend and indicates that God is willing to respond, even if the response is not, at first hearing, as comforting as we might hope.

God's Will

Even though we may know that God and God's ways are a mystery that only God can know, we still try to identify God's will in the workings of creation. Often when a catastrophe occurs, whether in the form of a natural disaster or a human evil, we hear people speak of God's will: "God willed this hurricane in order to strengthen us and to draw us closer to him." "God wanted your mother to die so that she would be happy in heaven, where she will watch over you." "God wills whatever happens to us for our good." An example of this is given in a letter that John of the Cross wrote to a nun who was experiencing great pain because she had been moved to another convent: "It is His Majesty who has done this, to bring you greater profit." Such explanations presume to know God's intention. I would prefer not to ascribe to God an intention I do not know, so suffering and evil remain a mystery that places me squarely before the question of who God is.

When we think of God as the ultimate fixer of everything, we get into trouble explaining natural disasters and human evil. God creates and sustains a world of shifting tectonic plates, complex climatic interactions, and other such phenomena that, at times, cause havoc in human lives. God does not intervene to stop the shifting of the plates or change climatic conditions. And when it comes to human evil, if God did not stop the crucifixion of Jesus, then perhaps God cannot change human hearts unless those hearts agree to change. God, of course, wants to influence our hearts, but God cannot coerce them to change.

The questions God poses at the end of the book of Job point to the immensity of the universe. At the heart of this immense universe is God, desiring it into existence and sustaining it at every moment. Why horrific things happen, such as the rape of a child, genetic abnormalities, and tsunamis, is part of the mystery of the universe. We may learn the scientific explanation of some of these phenomena, and we may learn, through this explanation, how to prevent some of them in the future, but the mystery will remain, because ultimately we can never know the mind of God. If we could, God would not be God.

What can we do when we are faced with the reality of pain and evil and cannot know why God allows them? Commenting on the letter of John of the Cross just cited, Iain Matthew notes that, for John, what turns pain into something ultimately positive is trust in God: "Grieve, address what can be addressed, do not condone the sin that may be causing the situation; but trust that the Father holds this situation in his hands, and will turn it into a blessing." I would add "Rage at God, if you feel like doing so." The trust that Matthew, citing John of the Cross, recommends comes from prior experience of God as the Creator who desires you and everyone else into existence for the sake of friendship. Sometimes, John of the Cross and Iain Matthew remind us, we find ourselves in situations that can only be endured with blind trust in the God we have met and come to believe in.

The experience of others who trusted God amid horrors may help us understand this response. I have met people who have found such trust, and you probably have as well. John of the Cross came to his conclusion about God through the ordeal of near-fatal harsh treatment and imprisonment by his own brother Carmelites. In such terrible circumstances, he found God's presence to be a sustaining, passionate love. During that ordeal, he wrote his love poems to God, poems that are considered classics in Spanish literature. He believed that he could not have known God so well without having experienced imprisonment.

Etty Hillesum, a Jewish woman who lived in Amsterdam during the Nazi occupation of the city, found God before dying at Auschwitz. On May 26, 1942, prior to her imprisonment, she wrote this prayer:

> It is sometimes hard to take in and comprehend, oh God, what those created in Your likeness do to each other in these disjointed days. But I no longer shut myself away in my room, God, I try to look things straight in the face, even the worst crimes, and to discover the small, naked human being amid the

monstrous wreckage caused by man's senseless deeds. I don't sit here in my peaceful flower-filled room, praising You through Your poets and thinkers. That would be too simple, and in any case I am not as unworldly as my friends so kindly think. Every human being has his own reality, I know that, but I am no fanciful visionary, God, no schoolgirl with a "beautiful soul." I try to face up to Your world, God, not to escape from reality into beautiful dreams—though I believe that beautiful dreams can exist beside the most horrible reality—and I continue to praise Your creation, God, despite everything.

As her train left Holland for Auschwitz, Hillesum tossed out a note that read, "We have left the camp singing." Isn't it amazing that these words could have been written in the midst of such horror?

In the end, we don't need to understand evil; we just need to say yes to God. A Portuguese proverb says that God writes straight with crooked lines. God, we believe, wrote straight with the crooked line of the rejection of the Messiah. God, we trust, writes straight with all the crooked lines that touch so many human lives throughout history. More, we cannot know of the mystery of evil; more, we do not need to know if we trust that God truly is our friend—or, as a Portuguese translation of the book of Wisdom has it, truly "amigo da vida," friend of life (11:26). Speaking of the "dark night" of John of the Cross, Iain Matthew writes, "But for night to be . . . blessed, there needs also, at some level, to be a 'yes.'" Life does throw us any number of curveballs, terrible things that are hard to handle, but if we want to find some measure of peace and blessing, we must say yes as Jesus did in the Garden of Gethsemane: "Abba, Father, for you all things are possible; remove this cup from me; yet, not what I want, but what you want" (Mark 14:36).

The prophet Habakkuk seems to have been able to say yes to God in spite of great calamities. We might ask God to help us say something like this:

> Though the fig tree does not blossom,
>   and no fruit is on the vines;
> though the produce of the olive fails
>   and the fields yield no food;
> though the flock is cut off from the fold
>   and there is no herd in the stalls,
> yet I will rejoice in the LORD;
>   I will exult in the God of my salvation.
>   (3:17–18)

God Has Shared Our Lot

Our objection to the idea of friendship with God because of the ideas explored here might be tempered by one final thought. Christians believe that Jesus of Nazareth is God incarnate. In him, God participated in the lot of all humans.

Jesus' parents were forced to leave their home in Nazareth for Bethlehem for a Roman census while Mary was very close to childbirth. In Bethlehem, Jesus was born in a stable. The young family was forced into exile in Egypt to escape the madness of King Herod. Jesus, it seems, lost his father, Joseph, sometime before Jesus began his public ministry. Finally, the leaders of his own religion handed him over to the Roman occupiers to die a horrible death. God is no stranger to suffering. God, in Jesus, knows what human life is like from the inside. God's desire for friendship with us knows no bounds. Our friend wants to share everything with us, even those things that make us angry and resentful of God.

» 11

How Am I to Understand God's Anger and Justice?

One thought that keeps coming back to me, and may have occurred to you, is that God is a just God, and the Bible speaks often of God's anger at the injustices and sins of the people. The way I have talked throughout this book about God's love and desire for friendship seems to ignore the passages in Scripture referring to God's anger and justice. Am I being too sunny in my expectations about God? Moreover, in focusing on friendship with God, aren't we in danger of accepting the status quo in our world? The world is not the way God wants it to be. How does God react to our sins and acts of injustice and still draw us into friendship?

If you are troubled by these questions, you are not alone. Let's take a stab at a response in this meditation.

God's Anger

When we consider instances of God's anger in the Bible, we can be tempted to interpret it literally. But it is important to realize that the Scriptures, while inspired by God, were written by human beings who carried the same psychological, sociological, and cultural baggage that affects how we experience God. They brought their hopes and fears to bear on what they believed of God, just as we do.

If you asked yourself whether the God you have experienced recently would sanction ethnic cleansing, you would probably quickly answer no, but there are many people, Christian and non-Christian, who would disagree with you. They believe that God is on their side and wants them to protect themselves against their enemies by any means at their disposal, including genocide. We have been witnesses of such a belief in our own times—in Nazi Germany, in Rwanda, in the former Yugoslavia, and in many other places. The Israelites of the Bible at one time believed that God wanted them to wipe out everyone in the Promised Land into which God was leading them from Egypt. Only gradually did they come to believe that God wants all people to live in peace and harmony, the message of the great prophecies of Isaiah that we read during Advent.

In a religion that believed that everything happened because God wished it, it was easy for prophets to proclaim that the calamities that came upon the people were

God's wrathful responses to their infidelities. It is, however, possible to interpret these calamities as the result of failed political policies. Israel at times made alliances with countries that eventually lost the power to protect them. For example, the prophet called First Isaiah warned Israel's leaders against trusting in an alliance with Egypt, but they did not heed him. When Egypt weakened and Assyria and Babylon grew in power, the Israelites paid dearly for their folly with the destruction of Jerusalem and the Babylonian exile. But was this payment punishment from God directly or just the result of trusting in a human power to protect their sovereignty? Eventually, every empire begins to weaken, and those who have been oppressed tend to seek vengeance.

These historical reflections suggest that we should exercise some caution in what we attribute to God's intention, even in biblical stories and prophecies. If God does not act in vengeful anger, how does God respond to injustice?

How God Reacts to Human Folly and Sin

We have been reflecting on the world as God's family business and on God's desire for the world. Clearly human beings have not fully heeded God's desire. Violence, hatred, war, and destruction of the environment seem to rule the day. How does God react to what human beings have made of the family business? You can ask God this question and then compare the response you receive with the response

I received from God. Perhaps together we can get some inkling of how God's justice and mercy cohabit.

When I asked God, this is what came to me in prayer: "How do you react when you are in my presence, especially when you know that you have sinned? Do you think anyone could be in my presence and remain untouched?" I realized that in such circumstances, I felt shame and sorrow and asked for the grace to avoid that sin in the future. I did not sense that God was angry with me, but I could not have lived in God's presence without acknowledging my failures and sins and repenting of them.

As I reflected on this, it came to me that no matter how heinous the crimes we commit, if we allow ourselves to become aware of God's presence, we will feel called to repentance and sorrow. We cannot be aware of God and not be aware of how short we have fallen of the person God calls us to be. In fact, it seems to me that people might be so shocked by the utter goodness and holiness of God that they would, at least at first, want to run away and hide. I believe that their shock and fear would come not because God was terrifyingly angry, but because they felt so unholy and unworthy. They might expect anger and rejection and perhaps even feel rejected, but that would be their own projection onto God; they would interpret God's utter love, holiness, and mercy as anger because they felt so unworthy. But if they stayed in God's presence, they would feel embraced by love and forgiveness and want to express their sorrow and repentance. They would also desire to change their lives and realize that they could do so only with the help of this God of love and forgiveness.

The seventeenth-century English poet George Herbert expressed well in "Love (III)" what often goes on in us sinners when we encounter the holiness of God:

> Love bade me welcome: yet my soul drew back,
>   Guilty of dust and sin.
> But quick-eyed Love, observing me grow slack
>   From my first entrance in,
> Drew nearer to me, sweetly questioning
>   If I lacked anything.
>
> "A guest," I answered, "worthy to be here":
>   Love said, "You shall be he."
> "I, the unkind, ungrateful? Ah, my dear,
>   I cannot look on thee."
> Love took my hand, and smiling did reply,
>   "Who made the eyes but I?"
>
> "Truth, Lord; but I have marred them; let my shame
>   Go where it doth deserve."
> "And know you not," says Love, "who bore the
>   blame?"
>   "My dear, then I will serve."

> "You must sit down," says Love, "and taste my
>   meat."
>   So I did sit and eat.

Herbert expresses our confusion and shame and our expectation of rebuff when we come into the presence of God. But we discover, as he did, that God invites us to a common meal of friendship. Blessed Julian of Norwich, the fourteenth-century English hermit, remarked after one of her experiences of God, "But it seems to me that there can be no anger in God, for our good Lord is always thinking of his own glory and the good of all who shall be saved."

I am trying to describe something difficult to fathom. God is love and compassion, but God, you might say, also has standards. When we are in God's presence, we become aware that we have not lived as we were created to live, as the image and likeness of God. These are the standards I mean. We know that we have not been compassionate toward those in need; we have not been poor in spirit, or meek, or honest, or kind, or trusting. Often we have been just the opposite of what we were created to be. We have lived a "false self," as described by Thomas Merton. In the presence of the Holy One, we become aware of how false and unholy we are, we who were created to be perfect as our heavenly Father is perfect (Matthew 5:48). But at the same time, if we can stand the honesty required in this holy Presence, we also recognize that we are being offered forgiveness and an opportunity for repentance and conversion.

Recall the experience of Rebecca Ann Parker mentioned in chapter 9. In a therapy session, she was able to go back to the time when, at four years of age, she was raped by a neighbor. In that session, she realized that she had been sustained as a child by a Presence and that the rapist could not have continued doing what he was doing if he became aware of that Presence. As I read Parker's account, I did not get the impression that the Presence was anything but loving and sustaining. She does not say that the Presence was loving and caring toward her and at the same time ready to destroy the rapist.

This is what I realized when I asked God about God's anger. What realizations did you come to? It would be a great grace for us to talk about our experiences. I hope that you can find people with whom to share what you have experienced.

God's Justice

The God who desires our friendship also desires the friendship of all human beings and their cooperation in developing a world that can sustain all of God's friends. God wants a just world, a world where men and women are in right relationships with one another as well as with God, where all are cared for. How does God react to our world? I sense that there is more to say on the question of God's justice in the face of the massive injustices we human beings have created.

Our world is sown with injustice, and its fruits are pervasive. Too often we do not see, or do not allow ourselves to see, these fruits. But at times the veil of our ignorance is pulled aside, and then we see that we live in a world of social injustice. In the United States, Hurricane Katrina lifted the veil of ignorance for many of us as we saw thousands of poor African Americans in New Orleans bear the brunt of its effects. Many people responded with great charity to what they saw on television, but most of us did not take the next step and address the systemic injustices that keep poor African Americans (and the poor in general) at the bottom of the social class system.

I don't want to get on a soapbox here, because I don't think that diatribes help us face the realities of our world with the kind of compassion and dedication that are needed to change social structures. Instead I suggest that each of us read the newspaper for a week while asking God to help us see our world through God's eyes. We might return to the suggestion made by Ignatius of Loyola in his contemplation on the Incarnation in *The Spiritual Exercises*. Ignatius has us imagine the Trinity looking at our world and deciding to send the Son. Ask God to help you read the news from the perspective of the Trinity.

As you contemplate the news from God's perspective, what do you experience? I sense God's sadness that there is so much violence and misery among us. "It's not what I want," I can hear God say. "What will you do to make a difference?" Sometimes I feel helpless and angry, but these feelings lead only to blaming others, and I realize that I am looking for scapegoats so that I can erase my complicity in these social ills and my responsibility to get involved. What have I done to change the political climate so that more people will want to support policies that move my city, my state, and my country toward a more just and equitable society? In other words, I realize that I am part of the problem and need to be converted in order to do what I can to change public policy.

In *Raising Abel*, the theologian James Alison tells an imaginative story of a now-aged Cain in his tent trying to sleep. He has never had much peace of mind as he has wandered the world, always fearing reprisal for killing his brother, Abel. He wakes from a fitful sleep sensing that someone has entered his tent and is looking at him. He realizes that it is his brother, and Cain expects to be killed. Instead, he hears the words "Fear not, it is I, your brother, do you not remember?" Abel helps Cain remember. Alison writes:

> This process of remembering his brother is not all pleasant for the old man, since at every awakening to what had really happened, it shakes him to see what it was that had been driving him since then, what strange and fatal mechanisms of love and hatred interlaced; and his whole story of wandering, of searching for shelter,

of killing and driving out to protect himself, all stand revealed as unnecessary. At every step his brother allows him to see what had really been going on, and at each step the old man would like to do what his leathern'd legs will no longer allow him to do: to flee before hearing more, so much does he fear the turning inside out of everything he has come to be.

Nevertheless, the young brother doesn't let him off this strange trial, strange, for in this court, the younger brother is victim, attorney, and judge, and the trial is the process of unblaming the one who did not dare to hear an accusation that never comes. Strangely, as his memory takes body, the old man begins to feel less and less the weight of the threatened end, which he had almost heard roaring about his ears. And he was right to lose that feeling, for the end has already come, but not as a threat: it has come as his brother who forgives him.

This imaginative trial appealed to me because it felt like what happens when we are in the presence of God. We *are* judged; that is, we do have to face honestly the reality of what we have done or left undone. This is God's justice, but we realize that God's justice is love and forgiveness. We do not need to fear God's presence. We are freed by God's judgment, and if it is not the judgment we all face after our death, it leads to a desire to change and to do what we can to make our world more like the world God wants.

How does this strike you? Does it square with your own experience of contemplating the world through God's eyes? Perhaps you, too, can say with the psalmist, "Love and truth will meet; justice and peace will kiss" (85:11, NAB). Once again, I hope you have people with whom you can talk about your experience. If not, perhaps you can, like Mary at the Annunciation, treasure all these things in your heart (Luke 2:51).

» 12

Does God Reveal the Divine Inner Life to Us?

I have stressed mutual self-revelation as one of the central hallmarks of friendship. With my best friends, I want to be as honest as I can be about my inner life, especially as it bears on our friendship, and I hope that they will reciprocate. Is there something analogous to this mutual self-revelation in our friendship with God? Does God reveal the divine inner life to us? Or does the analogy break down at this point? After all, one thing seems to be clear: if human beings think they comprehend God, they are wrong. God is an unfathomable mystery; everything we say positively about God must be negated in the same breath. Otherwise, we make God into a puzzle to be solved. When we see God face-to-face, it will be our delight, I believe, to realize that we can never fathom the divine Mystery.

On the other hand, Christians profess that God is triune and speak of three Persons in one God. Is this the revelation of God's inner life? If it is, it must have some meaning for our lives and our friendship with God.

In this meditation, I want to talk about this revelation insofar as it has a bearing on God's desire for our friendship. This will not be easy to discuss or to comprehend. If ever we needed God's help during the course of this book, it is now. I don't want to lead you astray or bore you with theological theory. Perhaps the difficulty of saying something intelligible about God's self-revelation says something about who God is.

A Revelation in Deeds

There is no place in Scripture where we are told point-blank that God is triune. Yet God *has* revealed something about the divine inner life that led to the doctrine of the Trinity. This revelation, however, like most deep self-revelations, did not come so much in words as in deeds—deeds of God in the history of the Hebrew people, in the person of Jesus, and in the work of the Spirit in human history. Of course, this revelation in deeds did not remove the veil of God's mystery, no more than human self-revelation in deed or word removes the veil of human mystery. No matter how deeply my closest friend reveals herself to me, she remains a mystery. If this is true of human friendship, how much more true is it of friendship with God?

That the world exists at all reveals something about God. God does not need the universe in order to be God. When we come to the awesome awareness that our world, and we in it, exist only because God wants our existence, we can begin to reflect on the One who does this. In creating the universe, God reveals God's self, since there is nothing else that could be a model. But we have to allow ourselves to be intrigued by the mystery that "there is anything, anything at all," as Denise Levertov put it in "Primary Wonder."

In an essay exploring the theology of the Trinity, Rowan Williams, the archbishop of Canterbury, writes: "As creatures, existing because of the utterance of God, we know that God desires to be God *for* what is not God— desires the pleasure or flourishing of what is not God." Unlike our desire, God's desire is not piqued by the existing attractiveness of anything; nothing exists until God wants it. Creating what is not God does not "assist God in being God," as Williams says. "What God utters . . . is God: the summons to the world to be, and to find its fruition in being in the presence of God, sets 'outside' God the kind of life that is God's." In other words, God creates what God is, but the life created exists "outside" of God. I presume that Williams puts quotation marks around *outside* because this spatial metaphor does not really work; nothing is "outside" God, because God is not spatial. But Williams shows that in creating a universe, God reveals Godself, because there is nothing else to reveal.

So what is revealed about God with creation? There is something about God's inner life that is self-giving. Williams puts it this way: "It seems we must say that God is already one whose being is a 'being for,' whose joy is eternally in the joy of another." Within God—apart from creation—there is "joy in the joy of another."

Neither Williams nor anyone else would have come to the notion that within God there is "joy in the joy of another" if another "deed" of God had not happened in the world—namely, the Incarnation. In chapter 4, we contemplated the life, death, and resurrection of Jesus of Nazareth, a Jew of the first century of our era. We came in touch with a human being like us in all things but sin who nonetheless provoked the same kind of awe in his first disciples and in Christians for centuries that the presence of God provokes. Jesus came to a human knowledge of himself that could have made him wonder about his sanity: he believed that he was one with the Mystery he called "dear Father." Either he was a madman or charlatan or he was the Son of God in a unique sense that could only mean he was the presence of God as a human being. In the life, death, and resurrection of Jesus of Nazareth, God reveals an inner life that is in some mysterious way relational. Jesus calls God "Abba," yet in deed and word he also evinces a oneness with God that is true of no other creature. So in God there are at least two who are One. We can use the word *persons* to point to the two as long as we define *person* only in terms of relation without implying two different beings.

What seems to have happened in the early Christian church is that the people noticed that their experience of awe and delight and fear in the presence of God, YHWH, was similar to their experience in the presence of the risen Jesus and in their remembered experience of Jesus before he died. Moreover, because of Jesus' life, death, and resurrection, they were becoming a different kind of human community. Both Jesus' resurrection after his humiliating crucifixion and their own rebirth into a forgiven, forgiving, and inclusive community could only be ascribed to the action of God. So Jesus was not crazy or a charlatan, but must have been, must be, who he indicated he was, the Son of God in a unique way, God's bodily presence on this earth.

The early church recalled that Jesus had spoken of sending his Spirit. Their own transformation into a new way of being human could only have come about by the presence of God active in them as individuals and as a community. In this activity, God revealed that the relationality within God was threefold. This is how the people experienced God's friendship. They received the revelation of God as Trinity not through some esoteric doctrine given to them as initiates in a special cult, but through God's saving action in creating and redeeming our world—hence, God reveals who God is in deeds more than words.

If you engaged in the exercises suggested in chapters 4 and 5 on friendship with Jesus and the Spirit, you may have experienced something similar to what the early Christians experienced. If so, then you have some experiential knowledge of the threeness of the one God. This knowledge is "heart knowledge." Something has happened to you, and you know that you have experienced God present and active in Jesus of Nazareth and in the renewed life that is the gift of the Spirit. You have experienced the creating, redeeming, and saving presence of God, whom Christians name Father, Son, and Holy Spirit.

Moreover, just as we experienced in Jesus' life and death the compassionate vulnerability of God, so, too, as we live life in the Spirit, we experience the compassionate vulnerability of God who is Father, Son, and Spirit. The Spirit is not coercive; the Spirit's action in us moves us to become more forgiving, more compassionate, and more inclusive in our relationships. But we can, and very often do, refuse to follow these promptings. The very fact that the Spirit is the least mentioned Person of God indicates God's willingness to become the forgotten One in order to move us to become the human beings and the human community God creates us to be. God's self-revelation is all of a piece. God is the compassionate One who abases self in order to win us over to friendship.

PART III

Experiencing God

» 13

Where Do We Experience God?

If God wants our friendship, where do we experience God drawing us into such a relationship? So far, I have suggested taking time to pray in an effort to recognize such experiences, but it may also help to spend some time reflecting on where you have experienced God. In this chapter, I will explore with you various places where people have found God. We will together discover, I hope, that God can be found wherever we are. All we need to do is pay attention. Let's begin with some biblical moments of finding God.

While tending his father-in-law's sheep, Moses noticed something extraordinary: a bush burning but not being consumed. When he went for a closer look, he heard a voice saying: "Come no closer! Remove the sandals from your feet, for the place on which you are standing is holy ground" (Exodus 3:5). This is one of many incidents in the Bible where people felt the closeness of God—where, in a sense, heaven and earth met. This meeting happened again and again—at Mount Sinai, where God gave Moses the Ten Commandments; in the tent containing the Ark of the Covenant, which housed the commandments; and in Solomon's temple, with its Holy of Holies containing the Ark. As long as the temple stood, the Israelites felt some assurance that God was with them. The remaining wall of the destroyed Second Temple is called the Wailing Wall because the place of God's presence is no more, and Jews mourn God's absence.

God's place and our place were not totally separate for the Israelites; somehow they overlapped, and at certain times and places, human beings realized this overlap. God is not "out there" beyond this world, although at the same time God is not so "here" that creation and God are one. Theologians have coined the term *transcendence* to describe the "not-here-ness" of God and *immanence* to describe God's "here-ness."

For Christians, Jesus of Nazareth is now *the* place where heaven and earth meet, where the holy is present uniquely and forever. The baptism of Jesus (Luke 3:21–22) and his transfiguration (Mark 9:2–13) exemplify how heaven and earth meet in him. In Jesus, God is so present that he is, in some mysterious way, both fully human and fully divine. To meet Jesus is to meet God. Jesus is "holy ground" par excellence.

This chapter asks the question, where do we experience God? Where is our "holy ground"? The Irish speak of "thin places," where the border between heaven and earth, sacred and secular, seems especially porous and God is believed to "leak through" more easily. Because I believe that God can "leak through" anywhere, I prefer to say that in such places people find the presence of God more easily. Where are the thin places in your life? What makes a place thin? I want to reflect on these questions with you in this meditation.

Thin Places

The Jesuits of the New England Province have a retreat house at Eastern Point, on the rocky coast of the Atlantic in Gloucester, Massachusetts. For fifty years, people have been coming to this place to "find God," or to let themselves be found by God. The setting is magnificent. The main house is a stone mansion constructed in the early twentieth century. It faces the Atlantic Ocean just outside Gloucester Harbor. Sunrises are often stunning, and on clear days there is a special glow over the ocean at sunset. After a heavy storm at sea, the waves crash against the huge rocks at the edge of the property, sending water and spray fifty feet into the air, a thrilling sight and sound. The atmosphere of the retreat house itself is warm, silent, and peaceful. I have been privileged to direct young Jesuits from around the world in the thirty-day Spiritual Exercises of St. Ignatius of Loyola in this setting for the past ten years. These retreats take place at the beginning of autumn, for many the most spectacular season of the year in our region.

Many have experienced Eastern Point as a thin place. I mention it to encourage you to recall your own thin places. Where have you been "surprised by joy," to borrow the words of C. S. Lewis—surprised by the desire for God?

I believe that all of us have experienced such thin places in our lifetimes. Since medieval times, people have been drawn to the great cathedrals of Europe, especially to the cathedral in the small French town of Chartres, because they give promise of being such thin places. Millions of people over the centuries have walked famous pilgrimage trails, such as the five-hundred-mile pilgrimage from the French-Spanish border to Santiago de Compostela in Spain, because of stories of how others have found God on these pilgrimages.

What is it about these places and the ones you have found that makes them special?

Something in these places surprises you, captures your attention, and makes you forget your own concerns and worries. For a moment or longer, you become a contemplative in the primitive sense of the term: you pay attention to something or someone outside yourself. In fact, in some way you lose yourself in that something or someone. The sunrise over the ocean captures all of your attention, for example, and for that time you are not aware of the pain in your buttocks or how cold your ears have become or anything else. In such moments, God has a chance to break through the "problems insoluble and problems offering / their own ignored solutions" that "jostle for my attention," as Denise Levertov put it in "Primary Wonder." This ability to grab our attention is what makes certain places thin.

When people tell me that they have a hard time praying, I often suggest that they do something they like to do to take their minds off their ordinary cares and concerns. I recall one elderly nun who told me that she hated retreats because they were so boring. When I asked her what she liked to do, she mentioned crossword puzzles and walking in the woods. I suggested that she do this and see what happened. After a few days, she said with a wry smile that she was enjoying this retreat, and then, more shyly, she said that God seemed to be enjoying it, too. In another example, a young seminarian found himself very distracted in prayer. He told me that he liked to look at the architecture of the city in which he lived. When I suggested that he do this for his prayer, he said that he would feel guilty. So I said, "Well, pray any way you want to, but the next time you look at the architecture of the city, ask God to go with you, and tell me what happens." It was the beginning for him of a new way of relating to God. Both of these people found thin places, places where they forgot themselves for a time and gave God a chance to break into their consciousness.

We should be aware of the thin places in our lives, because they make experiences of God's creative desire for each one of us, and our correlative desire for God, more

> I want them to water-ski
> across the surface of a poem
> waving at the author's name on the shore.
>
> But all they want to do
> is tie the poem to a chair with rope
> and torture a confession out of it.
>
> They begin beating it with a hose
> to find out what it really means.

I can imagine God saying the same thing about the way we often use Scripture. Frequently, we don't let the Scriptures do what they were written to do—namely, to give the Mystery we call God a chance to be heard and met. The Bible is not a theological textbook designed only to feed our minds and provide intellectual insight. Most of the Bible is imaginative literature meant to draw us into its world so that God can touch us. Even the historical books are written as stories to touch our imaginations. The biblical writers want to help us encounter God; ultimately, they want to move us to engage personally with God. The story of Exodus, for instance, was written to capture the imaginations of the Israelites so that they would know in their bones how much God loved them; thus, they would learn to rely on God in the here and now and to call on God to remember the covenant God made with them at Sinai.

Liturgy as a Thin Place

When people gather together to celebrate their communion with God, it can be experienced as a thin place. There is something about the gathering of people for prayer, especially if they come from diverse families and backgrounds, that sets off sparks in those present, giving them a sense that they are on "holy ground." For Christians, of course, the Eucharist is the gathering that most often is experienced as "holy ground." Even ordinary, seemingly humdrum Eucharistic liturgies can touch those present with a sense of peace and communion that is both awesome and delightful, and they feel one with the Mystery we call God. This is all the more true when the Eucharist is celebrated with striking beauty and prayerfulness. If, in addition, the congregation is large and culturally and racially diverse, the experience can be even more moving, because we sense that God's dream— for a world in which all are one in friendship with God and one another—is being fulfilled.

Married and Family Life as Thin Places

My first draft of this chapter did not mention married and family life as possible thin places, which is probably typical of celibate thinking. I realized the lacuna when I read the essay "Marital Spirituality" by the married theologian Thomas Knieps-Port le Roi. He points out that the usual models of spirituality tend to presume a celibate way of life as the norm and to relegate married life to a kind of second-class status. I invite readers who are married to reflect on your married and family life to see where you have experienced God. Perhaps you will be helped in your reflection by these words of Knieps-Port le Roi:

> A spirituality proper to lay people, and especially to married people, will be growing in a different soil and will therefore bring forth different fruits. The soil is the whole range of what the couple experience together: daily routine, moments of intimate exchange, the taking of decisions about the life they will be leading together. There is no need for anyone to go in quest of this reality; in each marital relationship it is immediately there to be seen. The only question is how it can be developed so that it becomes something significant for faith and for the spiritual life. Or, to put it another way: how can the Spirit be discovered within this reality, the Spirit who makes the couple co-workers and friends with God?

A spirituality for laypeople can be developed only by laypeople who work it out in a dialogue with tradition and their own experience. One way forward is to hear from couples and their children how married and family life provide thin places.

Nature as a Thin Place

The poet Mary Oliver seems to have been born a contemplative. Read any of her many books of poetry, and you will find someone who pays attention to the world around her. Take, for example, "The Summer Day," with its haunting final question:

> Who made the world?
> Who made the swan, and the black bear?
> Who made the grasshopper?
> This grasshopper, I mean—
> the one who has flung herself out of the grass,
> the one who is eating sugar out of my hand,
> who is moving her jaws back and forth instead of up
>   and down—
> who is gazing around with her enormous and
>   complicated eyes.
> Now she lifts her pale forearms and thoroughly
>   washes her face.
> Now she snaps her wings open, and floats away.
> I don't know exactly what a prayer is.
> I do know how to pay attention, how to fall down
> into the grass, how to kneel down in the grass,

how to be idle and blessed, how to stroll through the
    fields,
which is what I have been doing all day.
Tell me, what else should I have done?
Doesn't everything die at last, and too soon?
Tell me, what is it you plan to do
with your one wild and precious life?

Oliver says that she does not know what a prayer is, but her attention to the tiny details of nature brings her to the posture of prayer: kneeling in the grass, feeling idle and blessed, aware that she has been given only "one wild and precious life." When I have used this poem in retreats, it has helped people pay attention to God's creation and, in that attention, find God.

Oliver's book *Thirst* contains the poem "Praying," which gives a little instruction on how to pray with nature:

It doesn't have to be
the blue iris, it could be
weeds in a vacant lot, or a few
small stones; just
pay attention, then patch

a few words together and don't try
to make them elaborate, this isn't
a contest but the doorway

into thanks, and a silence in which
another voice may speak.

That's what thin places are all about: they lead us to put a few words together to address the Mystery, and they bring us to a silence "in which / another voice may speak."

Unlikely Thin Places

Mary Oliver's reference to "weeds in a vacant lot" brings to mind some unlikely places for finding God. Not all thin places are places of beauty and light and hope. My sister Mary, a Sister of Mercy, has worked for close to forty years in a home for troubled boys. At the end of a retreat at Eastern Point Retreat House, the retreatants were invited to speak of their experiences. A number of people spoke of finding God in the beauty of the place, in sunrises and sunsets, in the blue of the ocean, and on and on—in other words, in the "blue iris." Mary said that she too had had such experiences, but she went on to speak of seaweed that at first had seemed quite ugly to her. As she contemplated this seaweed, she began to see lovely colors in the ugly mess. It reminded her of how she often found grace and loveliness in the troubled boys with whom she works, who, at first glance, seemed unlovely and unlovable. Mary discovered thin places in seaweed and her boys. I invite you to think of some thin places that stand in opposition to the "blue iris" places.

Some places are so horrible that they grab our attention the way places of great beauty do. I can still remember my visit over fifty years ago to the concentration camp in Dachau, just outside Munich, Germany. What stands out in my memory is the word *Badezimmer* (Bathroom) over the door to the room where men, women, and children were gassed to death. They had been told to leave their clothes outside the room so they could be deloused in a shower. But instead of water, poison gas burst from the pipes. I imagined their horror as they realized what was happening. How could human beings do such things to other human beings?

At the time, I was just numb. I believe that I began to cry. I do not remember any sense of God. I wanted to get out of there as soon as possible. Perhaps the ugliness and horror hit me so strongly that I missed the opportunity to let Dachau become a thin place for me. Perhaps many of us miss the thinness of such places of horror because we cannot or do not want to stay long enough to let them become places where we can meet God.

Can you think of times when you found your heart burning with something mysterious while you were in an unlikely place? You may have felt something like this in the presence of someone you love who was dying. Recently, one of my Jesuit friends told me of a visit his sister made to their dying brother, who radiated such peace and joy that she felt lifted up herself. This was an unlikely thin place.

The theologian Belden Lane found an unlikely thin place in the nursing home where his mother was dying of cancer and Alzheimer's disease. When she tried to rip out her feeding tube, he had to call for help, which led to his mother having to wear mittens. He writes:

> There she lay—miserable, stripped of dignity, incapable of helping herself in the least way—and now betrayed by a son whose best intentions had only made things worse. I left the room, choking on my own helplessness.
>
> But the unexpected occurred that afternoon when I returned to the nursing home. My mother was resting quietly by then, the gloves removed. She looked up and said to me gently, in an unusual moment of lucidity, "Don't cry, Belden. It's natural to have to do this. It's all a part of dying." With those words a window suddenly opened. By an unanticipated grace, I found healing through the one I'd meant to comfort.

Perhaps you, too, have found a thin place at a time of difficult ministry, such as the terrible day experienced by the chaplain in the acute care unit of the large hospital mentioned in chapter 9. She found herself moved with compassion for a woman who may have shaken her baby to death. In the process of her ministry, the chaplain found herself present with God.

Sometimes an unlikely thin place is revealed by the people there who show the face of God. Auschwitz, the Nazi death camp in Poland, is one such place. Two canonized saints, Sister Teresa Benedicta of the Cross (Edith Stein) and Father Maximilian Kolbe, died there. Edith Stein, born a Jew, refused to try to escape to Switzerland from Holland when Jewish Christians were threatened with exportation to Auschwitz. In compassion for her people, she wanted to share their fate. The Franciscan priest Maximilian Kolbe volunteered to take the place of a man with a family who had been chosen to die in reprisal for an escape. These are only two of many instances of compassion that revealed the presence of God in this place of unimaginable horror. Even today, people who enter Auschwitz speak of experiencing God's presence.

You may recall other horrors either witnessed directly or through the media that became thin places for you. At the end of the documentary *Born into Brothels*, the story of how a gift of cameras allowed poor children of Calcutta to capture in film some of the horrors and joys of their lives, I was devastated to the point of tears by what these children had to endure and, at the same time, moved by their indomitable spirit. A colleague, Linda Amadeo, recalls her reactions to the film *Hotel Rwanda*, which depicts the horror of the genocide in Rwanda and the heroism of a hotel manager who saved so many Tutsi. She watched in numb silence and overwhelming sadness, often breaking down in sobs. She felt deep admiration for the manager; later, when she learned that the survivors are beginning to forgive those who perpetrated this atrocity, she felt astonished. Still later, she felt profound gratitude to God for loving us enough to redeem us despite what we do to one another. Only then came a little peace.

Of course, the unlikeliest thin place in all of history is Golgotha, where church and state conspired to kill an innocent man. Yet even here the Roman centurion who led the soldiers who crucified Jesus gasped, "Truly this man was God's Son!" (Mark 15:39). Ever since that awful and awesome day, Christians have contemplated Jesus on the cross and found God and hope and peace there. It is unlikely indeed, yet a fact!

I hope it has become clear how easily one can find places where heaven and earth meet, whether amid beauty or devastation, sorrow or joy. Perhaps these examples will spur you to spend time with your own "weeds in a vacant lot" to see if they have been thin places for you. God, who invites us to friendship, is present and active everywhere. As the Jesuit poet Gerard Manley Hopkins put it, "The world is charged with the grandeur of God." Every place on this earth can be a thin place. All that is required to experience God is our openness to God's presence.

» 14

How Do I Know I'm Experiencing God?

We have talked often in this book about how the Spirit moves us toward becoming images of God and how we can, and very often do, refuse to follow the Spirit's promptings. I want to address here the question of how we are to distinguish the promptings of the Spirit of God from the welter of promptings that beset us as we try to lead a human life. This brings us very close to the question of self-delusion, which has to unsettle anyone who is serious about the experience of God.

In the Old Testament, the question of self-delusion comes up in warnings about telling a true prophet from a false prophet. In the New Testament, the warning is repeated: "Beloved, do not believe every spirit, but test the spirits to see whether they are from God; for many false prophets have gone out into the world" (1 John 4:1). How do I know that I am not a false prophet, that what I have written in this book speaks at least some truth about God? How do you know that your experiences of God are actually of God? In this chapter, I will outline a process of "testing the spirits" in order to know whether one is on the right path toward God; in the history of spirituality, it is called the discernment of spirits.

An Experience of St. Ignatius of Loyola

Some presentations on the discernment of spirits make it seem beyond the reach of ordinary mortals. But the ability to discern the spirits is not limited to saints, mystics, and certain religious. Ignatius of Loyola began his long journey of discerning the various spirits that were moving him when he was almost clueless about the spiritual life.

Ignatius was an ambitious, hard-charging young noble when a cannonball shattered his legs. During his long recovery, he spent many hours daydreaming and reading the only books available in the Loyola castle: a life of Christ and a book of lives of the saints. In one set of daydreams, he imagined the great deeds he would do to win the favor of a great lady, and he enjoyed these imaginings immensely. When he read the life of Christ and some of the lives of the saints, he began to imagine the great deeds he would do in imitation of Jesus and the saints, and he enjoyed these daydreams as well. There was a difference, however, in his state after the two sets of daydreams. After the daydreams about the knightly deeds, he felt out of sorts, but after those about following Jesus, he continued to feel happy and content. For a long time, however, he did not pay attention to this difference, until one day his eyes were opened. He says in his *Reminiscences*:

> His eyes were opened a little, and he began to marvel at this difference in kind and to reflect on it, picking it up from experience that from some thoughts he would be left sad and from others happy, and little by little coming to know the difference in kind of spirits that were stirring: the one from the devil, and the other from God.

Ignatius began to learn how to discern the spirits through paying attention to his feelings while daydreaming. God and the evil spirit, Ignatius came to believe, were working in his daydreams to different ends. This story should remove some of the mystery associated with the term *discernment of spirits*.

Those of us who believe that God is present at every moment of the world's existence can hope to discern the movements inspired by God in every experience we have. The discernment of spirits is not limited to what happens when we pray formally. Ignatius's experience proves this.

Ignatius did not become an expert in discernment from that moment, but it was the beginning of his schooling of heart and mind to recognize God's activity in his experience and to differentiate it from the activity of the one Ignatius called "the enemy of human nature." Ignatius says that God led him the way a teacher might lead a schoolboy. Gradually, he became a master of discernment and formulated a series of rules for discernment of spirits, which are contained in his *Spiritual Exercises* (nn. 313–336). I will present here some of these rules in language for our time. I hope that they will help you discern what is of God in your experience.

It is important to note before we start that while our experience is the only place where we can encounter God, no experience is pure; every experience we have is influenced by what is outside us, by our psychological makeup, by our sociological and cultural background, by the language we speak, and by our bodily states. Every experience is multidimensional. An insightful comment by the Anglican theologian Martin Thornton gives an example of this multidimensionality:

> A rose, then, is by selection and interpretation, something different to different people. To the botanist it is *rosaceae arvensis*, to the gardener it is an Ena Harkness, to the aesthete a beautiful sight, and to the blind man it is a wonderful smell. . . . None of these have experienced the rose in its totality, but when Temple's religious man says that it is a creature of God which may disclose his presence, his interpretation is no less valid.

There are no pure experiences of a rose or of anything else; any experience is colored by our past experiences and our point of view.

Still, for believers every experience is influenced by God's Spirit. Hence, there is a religious dimension to every experience we have, at least for those of us who believe in the omnipresence of God. For those who believe in the evil spirit, that spirit can also influence experience. Given this mass of influences on our experience, we ask how to discern what is of God.

Guidelines for Discernment

Fortunately, in order to discern what is of God, we do not have to figure out all the influences—for example, what is due to what we ate for dinner or how we were brought up by our parents. Discernment of spirits does not require an archaeological dig through all the layers that make up every experience. We just need to pay attention to what we experience and then apply a few simple rules.

The Orientation of Your Life

In Ignatius's rules for the discernment of spirits, his first piece of advice is to ascertain the orientation of your life: Am I straying from the right path, or am I trying to live a decent Christian life? As a reader of this book, you should have an easy time answering this question! You would not be reading this if you were straying—that is, if you were turned against God and God's way. Scrupulous people may say that they are afraid they are on the road to hell, but the fact that they are trying so hard to make sure that they do not sin shows the fallacy of their assessment.

Rule One

Just to be complete, let me explain what Ignatius says about the different ways God's Spirit and the evil spirit operate with those who have deliberately and seriously turned away from God. The evil spirit tries to get such people to rationalize their behavior and attitudes: "I'm not such a bad guy. I may steal money, but it's only what I deserve for all that I have done for this company." "Compared to Helen, I'm a saint." "I take care of my wife and kids; my affair with Jane doesn't hurt them because they don't know." In other words, the evil spirit tries to douse the conscience pangs of anyone who is acting contrary to what is right. The pangs of conscience, on the other hand, come from God's Spirit. They do not attack us, but rather raise questions about our behavior: "Are you really happy acting this way?" "Don't you feel a twinge of regret when you come home to your wife and family after an evening with your mistress?"

A real example may help. I don't think I was deliberately turned from God, but my consumption of alcohol was troubling others and me. Still, I did not want to look at the issue. I remember telling myself things like "You need a drink to relax after a hard day," "You never lose a day's work because of drinking," and "Your health is good. It's not having that bad of an effect."

These were rationalizations induced by the bad spirit and by my own unwillingness to take an honest look at my alcohol consumption. On the other hand, I had recurring feelings that something was wrong. I wondered at times about what alcohol was doing to my health. I blushed with shame when I remembered how harsh I had been with someone after having a couple of drinks, or when one of my friends expressed concern about my drinking. I believe that God's Spirit was trying to get me to look seriously at my drinking habits and do something about them, and the evil spirit was just as happy to see things remain as they were.

Finally, by the grace of God, I paid attention to the good spirit. I mention this personal experience to show that discernment of spirits is not esoteric. It just means paying attention to our experience in order to live more in accord with the way of God.

Rule Two
Now let's take up the orientation of most of us, who are trying to live honestly and uprightly to the best of our ability. In this case, Ignatius says, the good and bad spirits act in ways *opposite* to how they act with those turned away from God's path. The bad spirit raises doubts and questions that cause inner turmoil and self-absorption, while the good

spirit tries to encourage us and to increase our peace, joy, faith, hope, and love.

If you are trying to live as a good Christian, you might have thoughts like these: "Who do you think you are—some kind of saint?" "Everyone else cuts corners in this office. What's the matter with you? Are you holier-than-thou?" "God doesn't have time for the likes of you." "Most people, even if they believe in God, don't try to live the way you do." Such questions and thoughts have only one aim, to trouble your spirit and keep you troubled and questioning. Moreover, you will notice that all the questions and doubts focus on you, not on God or God's people.

The good spirit, on the other hand, might inspire thoughts like these: "I'm genuinely happy with my decision to make amends with my estranged sister." "I wish that I had stopped drinking a long time ago. I'm much happier and healthier now, and easier to live with." "God seems so much closer to me since I began to take some time every day for prayer, and I feel less anxious and insecure." I hope you can see in your own experience how these two spirits have led you.

Here's an example. Some years ago, a woman had three days of very consoling prayer on her annual retreat. She felt close to God, happy, and full of life and faith. Then, on the fourth day, she told me, "This is too highfalutin for me. I need to spend time preparing for my classes instead of praying." The next day, she could not pray and was miserable.

When we looked at what had happened, it turned out that the closeness to God had frightened her. Instead of telling God that she was frightened, which would have continued the conversation, she let her feelings of unworthiness get in the way of her experience. The evil spirit used her fear of closeness to God to move her to focus on her classes instead of on her joyful prayer. The interruption in prayer did not lead her to prepare for her classes, but only to a miserable day in the retreat. This is how the bad spirit operates with those who are trying to lead a life in conformity with friendship with God.

In summary, if you are somehow out of tune with God in your life, God will try to move you to change, and you will feel pangs of conscience. These pangs of conscience, however, will not lead to anxious self-examination and self-absorption, but will gently point out where you have gone wrong. The bad spirit, or your own desire not to change your life, will whisper rationalizations, trying to convince you that nothing is wrong. On the other hand, if you are trying to live in tune with God, God's Spirit will console you and encourage you, but the bad spirit or your own fear of closeness with God will try to make you doubtful of your experience. One sign of this bad spirit is that you become self-centered, rather than centered on God and others.

Ignatius provides a good example of how the bad spirit works with someone on the right road. At one point he had the thought "And how are *you* going to be able to stand this life [of prayer and penance] the seventy years you're meant to live?" Ignatius quite rightly answered, "Can you promise me one hour of life?" Alcoholics know this temptation well, hence the advice of Alcoholics Anonymous to take things one day at a time.

Rule Three: Spiritual Consolation

Ignatius believed that God wants us to be happy and fulfilled and that the way to be happy and fulfilled is to be in tune with God's dream for the world and for us. In the terms of this book, the way to be happy and fulfilled is to accept God's offer of friendship and to live in accordance with that friendship. If we are trying to do this, according to Ignatius, "consolation" is the order of the day. This does not mean that life will be without pain and suffering; it means that God wants to be a consoling presence to us even in the inevitable pains and sufferings of life. Therefore, the agonies of scrupulous people cannot come from God, since they are trying to live a good life. Ignatius himself, after the first fervor following his conversion, had a terrible bout with scruples about confessing his past sins. Things got so bad that he contemplated suicide. He finally came to the conclusion that these scrupulous thoughts could not be from God and decided never to confess past sins again.

What, exactly, is consolation? Consolation refers to any experience of desire for God, of distaste for one's past sins, or of sympathy for Jesus or any other suffering person.

It refers, in other words, to "every increase in hope, faith, and charity, and every interior joy which calls and attracts one toward heavenly things and to the salvation of one's soul, by bringing it tranquility and peace in its Creator and Lord" (*The Spiritual Exercises*, n. 316). Paul's letter to the Galatians lists the fruit of the Spirit as "love, joy, peace, patience, kindness, generosity, faithfulness, gentleness, and self-control" (5:22–23). When you experience this group of movements in your being, you can be relatively sure that God's Spirit is moving you.

Rule Four: Spiritual Desolation

Desolation is the opposite of consolation. Ignatius gives these examples:

> Obtuseness of soul, turmoil within it, an impulsive motion toward low and earthly things, or disquiet from various agitations and temptations. These move one toward lack of faith and leave one without hope and without love. One is completely listless, tepid, and unhappy, and feels separated from our Creator and Lord. (*The Spiritual Exercises*, n. 317)

Provided that we are trying to live as friends of God, experiences of feeling out of sorts, ill at ease, anxious, unhappy, listless, and so on are experiences of desolation. They do not come from God.

If we are trying to live as friends of God, we can trust that our experience is of God's Spirit when we find ourselves more alive, more peaceful, more energized, and also more concerned about others than about ourselves as a result of the experience. These simple rules of thumb are not absolute guarantees that we are right or that our way of proceeding will succeed, but they give us some assurance that we are on the right path. If we follow the impulses of such experiences, we can move forward with confidence, trusting that God will continue to show us the way.

Another Ignatian Example

During Ignatius's time at Manresa, where he began to formulate the ideas that would become the Spiritual Exercises, he concluded that God was calling him to spend his life in Jerusalem helping souls. When Ignatius got to Jerusalem, the provincial superior of the Franciscans in charge of the Holy Land told him that he would have to leave because of the dangerous circumstances. But Ignatius held firm and said that he intended to stay and that no danger would deter him. When the provincial realized that Ignatius would not leave on his own accord, he told him that he would excommunicate him from the Catholic Church if he did not leave with the other pilgrims. Ignatius decided that "it was not the will of Our Lord that he should remain in these holy places." Ignatius, apparently, was proved wrong in his interpretation of the movements of God in him. But he had to follow the "consoling" experiences to the point where he met what was for him an immovable obstacle—namely, an authority in the Catholic Church who could excommunicate him—to fulfilling what he believed God wanted. He was a Catholic to the core and therefore could not believe that God would lead him to do something that would get him excommunicated.

For Ignatius, as for any Roman Catholic, personal discernment of spirits stands in healthy tension with authority, and unless it is clear that one would be abandoning God by obeying authority in a conflict such as Ignatius felt, then authority trumps personal discernment. But the point here is that Ignatius would not have discerned his true vocation without following the best lights he had and going to Jerusalem.

After this setback, Ignatius went back to Spain determined to study theology in order to be able to help souls. But he did not entirely give up his goal of going to Jerusalem, as became clear when he gathered the first companions who were to be, with him, the founders of the Society of Jesus. All of these companions, while students at the University of Paris with Ignatius, made the Spiritual Exercises and came to the same conclusion that God was calling them to go to Jerusalem, to live and work there. They vowed to do this, but with the proviso that if they could not get there within a year they would put themselves at the disposal of the pope. Because of warfare, they could not sail to Jerusalem in the time allowed, and so they went to Rome, where they asked Pope Paul III to allow them to form the Society of Jesus. Ignatius and his companions had to follow the impulses that they discerned as coming from God's Spirit and then see what happened. This is an example of trusting in experience but also letting events show whether the decision taken leads anywhere.

Rule Fourteen

Before I finish this short introduction to discernment of spirits, I want to mention one of the Ignatian rules of thumb that has served me well. Ignatius writes of the enemy of human nature using the tactics of a military commander besieging a city. The commander will try to find the weak spot in the defense and attack it. So, too, Ignatius reasons, the evil spirit picks out our weak spots and attacks them in an effort to drive us away from God's friendship (*The Spiritual Exercises*, n. 327).

Thus, if I am prone to self-doubt, my self-doubt will be the evil spirit's point of attack every time I feel close to God. I will wonder if I am fooling myself to think that God wants my friendship or that I could have discerned the spirits rightly, even though everything seems to be moving in the right direction. If I have a tendency to find self-confidence only when I am working, then anytime I take time for myself, even when it is necessary for my health, I may feel some anxiety, and I will begin to question my actions. Each of us has weak points in our personality. Self-knowledge can help us know when we are being sidetracked by the promptings of the bad spirit.

These simple rules will help you do your part to remain in the friendship God wants with you. You will also be helped, I might add, by having someone to whom you can talk honestly about your life so that you can discern with more confidence where you are in tune with God, and where not. Many more people now avail themselves of the help of a spiritual director to stay true to the friendship with God.

Conclusion

In chapter 7 of the book of Wisdom, we read, "For she [wisdom] is a breath of the power of God, / and a pure emanation of the glory of the Almighty" (7:25). The Hebrew word translated as "spirit" can also be translated as "wind" or "breath"; hence, wisdom is often understood by Christians as the Spirit of God. The writer continues, "Although she is but one, she can do all things, / and while remaining in herself, she renews all things; / in every generation she passes into holy souls / and makes them friends of God, and prophets" (7:27).

Throughout this book, I have maintained that God wants all human beings to be such "holy souls," and thus "friends of God, and prophets." I hope that you have experienced God's desire for your friendship and your corresponding desire to be God's friend. I am convinced that the only way to the fulfillment of God's dream for our world is for more and more human beings to accept God's offer of friendship and begin to live out the consequences.

If we accept God's offer and try to live as God's friends, we become partners with God in the family business of building the world described by the prophet Isaiah:

The wolf shall live with the lamb,

    the leopard shall lie down with the kid,

the calf and the lion and the fatling together,

    and a little child shall lead them.

The cow and the bear shall graze,

    their young shall lie down together;

    and the lion shall eat straw like the ox.

The nursing child shall play over the hole of the asp,

    and the weaned child shall put its hand on the

        adder's den.

They will not hurt or destroy

    on all my holy mountain;

for the earth will be full of the knowledge of the

    LORD

    as the waters cover the sea.

    (11:6–9)

God wants friendship with you and with me and with all our brothers and sisters in the world. Let's take the offer, shall we? Bless you all.

Notes

Introduction

Page xviii: *even terrifying* Rudolf Otto, *The Idea of the Holy: An Inquiry into the Non-rational Factor in the Idea of the Divine and Its Relation to the Rational*, trans. John W. Harvey (New York: Oxford University Press, 1976).

Chapter 1

Page 3: *"perfect friendship"* E. D. H. (Liz) Carmichael, *Friendship: Interpreting Christian Love* (London: T&T Clark International, 2004), 34.

Page 4: *friendship with himself and one another* Ibid., 35.

Chapter 2

Page 10: *medieval rabbi's story* I read this in *America* years ago but cannot trace the reference. Even if it is apocryphal, it fits the kind of story found in Jewish lore.

Page 15: *inhabit it* In a number of theological works based on the anthropological theories of the French historian and philosopher René Girard, James Alison writes of *inhabiting* a text. See *The Joy of Being Wrong: Original Sin through Easter Eyes* (New York: Crossroad, 1998), *Raising Abel: The Recovery of the Eschatological Imagination* (New York: Crossroad, 1996), and *Faith beyond Resentment: Fragments Catholic and Gay* (New York: Crossroad, 2001).

Page 17: *final editor* Each of the books of the Bible has its own history of coming to its final form. Many were fashioned from earlier oral traditions, some of which may have first been written down separately. In the case of the book of Genesis, there are a number of such traditions. The final editor of the text we now have put them together to form a coherent book.

Page 18: *call of a father to a child*   E. A. Speiser, *Genesis*, Anchor Bible (Garden City, NY: Doubleday, 1964), 25.

Page 19: *the friend of God*   I am indebted here to the Swiss Jesuit Christian Rutishauser, whose expertise is Jewish studies.

Page 22: love *and* like   James Alison, *On Being Liked* (New York: Crossroad, 2003).

Chapter 3

Page 33: *spiritual director*   A spiritual director is someone to whom you can talk about your experiences of relating to God. A spiritual director can be clergy or lay; the only requirement is that you trust him or her to help you with your relationship with God. Some training in the kind of spiritual conversation you need would also be helpful in such a director.

Page 37: *Philippa and the geranium*   P. D. James, *Innocent Blood* (London: Penguin, 1989), 255.

Chapter 4

Page 56: *Jesus' humanity*   N. T. Wright, "How Jesus Saw Himself," *Bible Review* 12, no. 3 (1996): 29.

Page 67: *"God" vanishes*   Rowan Williams, *On Christian Theology* (Oxford: Blackwell, 2000), 121.

Page 69: *Gandalf and Sam*   J. R. R. Tolkien, *The Lord of the Rings*, book 3, *The Return of the King* (New York: Ballantine, 1965), 283.

Chapter 6

Page 95: *to be a Jesuit today*   Documents of the 31st and 32nd General Congregations of the Society of Jesus, trans. John Padberg (St. Louis: Institute of Jesuit Sources, 1977), 401.

Page 95: *a factor in God's life* Iain Matthew, *The Impact of God: Soundings from St. John of the Cross* (London: Hodder & Stoughton, 1995), 33.

Chapter 8

Page 106: *"Rocky"* Daniel J. Harrington, *The Gospel of Matthew*, Sacra Pagina, vol. 1 (Collegeville, MN: Liturgical Press, 1991), 247–48.

Page 110: *I am called Yahweh* Oliver Davies, *A Theology of Compassion: Metaphysics of Difference and the Renewal of Tradition* (Grand Rapids, MI: William B. Eerdmans, 2003), vii.

Page 111: *maximum immigration policy* Iain Matthew, *The Impact of God: Soundings from St. John of the Cross* (London: Hodder & Stoughton, 1995), 73–74.

Chapter 9

Page 123: *the Presence* Rita Nakashima Brock and Rebecca Ann Parker, *Proverbs of Ashes: Violence, Redemptive Suffering, and the Search for What Saves Us* (Boston: Beacon Press, 2001), 209–12.

Page 123: *within Himself* St. Teresa of Ávila, *Interior Castle*, trans. and ed. E. Allison Peers (Garden City, NY: Doubleday, 1961), 194.

Chapter 10

Page 133: *Job's final response* Iain Matthew, *The Impact of God: Soundings from St. John of the Cross* (London: Hodder & Stoughton, 1995), 63.

Page 135: *turn it into a blessing* Ibid., 93.

Page 137: *despite everything* Etty Hillesum, *An Interrupted Life: The Diaries, 1941–1943, and Letters from Westerbork*, trans. Arnold J. Pomerans (New York: Henry Holt, 1996), 134–35.

Page 137: *left the camp singing* Ibid., xvi.

Page 138: *a "yes"* Matthew, *The Impact of God*, 86.

Chapter 11

Page 145: *"Love (III)"* George Herbert, in *The Norton Anthology of Poetry*, ed. Alexander W. Allison et al., 3rd ed. (New York: Norton, 1983), 268.

Page 146: *no anger in God* Julian of Norwich, *Revelations of Divine Love*, trans. Elizabeth Spearing (London: Penguin Books, 1998), 61.

Page 146: *false self* James Martin, *Becoming Who You Are: Insights on the True Self from Thomas Merton and Other Saints* (Mahwah, NJ: Paulist Press, 2006).

Page 150: *his brother who forgives him* James Alison, *Raising Abel: The Recovery of the Eschatological Imagination* (New York: Crossroad, 1996), 133–34.

Chapter 12

Page 156: *joy in the joy of another* Rowan Williams, *On Christian Theology* (Oxford: Blackwell, 2000), 73–74.

Chapter 13

Page 169: *co-workers and friends with God?* Thomas Knieps-Port le Roi, "Marital Spirituality: A Paradigm Shift," *The Way* 45, no. 4 (October 2006): 59–74.

Page 174: *the one I'd meant to comfort* Belden Lane, *The Solace of Fierce Landscapes: Exploring Desert and Mountain Spirituality* (New York: Oxford University Press, 1998), 31.

Chapter 14

Page 179: *the other from God* St. Ignatius of Loyola, *Personal Writings: Reminiscences, Spiritual Diary, Select Letters, including the Text of the Spiritual Exercises*, trans. Joseph A. Munitiz and Philip Endean (London: Penguin, 1996),

15. All further references to the *Reminiscences* will be to this edition.

Page 180: *interpretation is no less valid* Martin Thornton, *My God: A Reappraisal of Normal Religious Experience* (London: Hodder & Stoughton, 1974), 45.

Page 181: *what is of God* Those who want to learn more about the theory behind this can see my book *Spiritual Direction and the Encounter with God: A Theological Inquiry*, rev. ed. (Mahwah, NJ: Paulist Press, 2004). See especially chapter 3, "The Religious Dimension of Experience," and chapter 6, "A Theology of Discernment of Spirits."

Page 186: *one hour of life* Ignatius of Loyola, *Personal Writings*, 22.

Page 188: *remain in these holy places* Ibid., 35.

Page 191: *the help of a spiritual director* If you want information about spiritual directors in your area, you can contact Spiritual Directors International (www.sdiworld.org), an organization that maintains a directory of spiritual directors in various parts of the world.

Annotated Bibliography

Barry, William A. *God and You: Prayer as a Personal Relationship.* New York: Paulist Press, 1987. Many have found this small book helpful for the development of their relationship with God.

———. *What Do I Want in Prayer?* New York: Paulist Press, 1994. In this book, I take the reader through the Spiritual Exercises as a form of prayer to develop the relationship with God.

———. *With an Everlasting Love: Developing an Intimate Relationship with God.* New York: Paulist Press, 1999. I further develop the theme of relationship with God.

Carmichael, E. D. H. (Liz). *Friendship: Interpreting Christian Love.* London: T&T Clark International, 2004. I found this book very helpful as a scholarly development of the theme.

Davies, Oliver. *A Theology of Compassion: Metaphysics of Difference and the Renewal of Tradition.* Grand Rapids, MI: William B. Eerdmans, 2003. This is a dense and difficult read, but very rewarding for those who want to make the effort required.

Lane, Belden. *The Solace of Fierce Landscapes: Exploring Desert and Mountain Spirituality.* New York: Oxford University Press, 1998. The fierce landscapes discussed here include nursing homes.

Martin, James. *Becoming Who You Are: Insights on the True Self from Thomas Merton and Other Saints.* Mahwah, NJ: Paulist Press, 2006. This insightful book shows how the relationship with God brings us to our true selves.

202 « Annotated Bibliography

Matthew, Iain. *The Impact of God: Soundings from St. John of the Cross*. London: Hodder & Stoughton, 1995. Many people have found this book to be a great source for prayer.

Wright, N. T. *Simply Christian: Why Christianity Makes Sense*. San Francisco: HarperSanFrancisco, 2006. This is a brilliant and accessible introduction to Christianity as an answer to the hungers of the human heart.

————. *Evil and the Justice of God*. Downers Grove, IL: InterVarsity Press, 2006. I read this great book after I finished the chapter in my book on human evil and natural catastrophes. Wright is one of the great Christian scholars and writers alive today.

Acknowledgments continued from page iv:

"Primary Wonder" by Denise Levertov (p. xiii) is from *Sands of the Well* (New York: New Directions, 1996). Used with permission of New Directions.

"Preparations" by Franz Wright (pp. 91–92) is from *God's Silence* (New York: Knopf, 2006). Used with permission of the author.

"Annunciation" by Denise Levertov (pp. 114–16) is from *A Door in the Hive* (New York: New Directions, 1989). Used with permission of New Directions.

"Introduction to Poetry" by Billy Collins (pp. 166–67) is from *The Apple That Astonished Paris* (Fayetteville: University of Arkansas Press, 1988). Used with permission of the author.

"The Summer Day" by Mary Oliver (pp. 170–71) is from *New and Selected Poems* (Boston: Beacon Press, 1992). Used with permission of Beacon Press.

"Praying" by Mary Oliver (pp. 171–72) is from *Thirst* (Boston: Beacon Press, 2006). Used with permission of Beacon Press.

Parts of chapters 9 and 10 originally appeared in *America*, October 2, 2006, 25–27. Versions of chapters 10 and 13 appeared in *Human Development*, Summer 2007 and Winter 2007. Permission to reprint is gratefully acknowledged.